D1391633

FEASTING FOR FESTIVALS

Jan Wilson

Illustrated by Linda Herd

SANDY LANE BOOKS

Text copyright © 1990 Jan Wilson
Colour illustrations copyright © 1990 Linda Herd
Black and white illustrations copyright © Tony De Saulles

This edition published by
Sandy Lane Books
Sandy Lane West, Oxford, England
ISBN 0 7459 4006 4
Albatross Books Pty Ltd
ISBN 0 7324

First edition 1990
This edition 1995
10 9 8 7 6 5 4 3 2 1 0

All rights reserved

A catalogue record for this title is available
from the British Library

Printed and bound in Singapore

Acknowledgments

Stir up, O Lord, page 16, collect for the fifth Sunday before Christmas from *The Alternative Service Book 1980*; the marriage vows, page 88, from the Marriage Service in *The Alternative Service Book 1980* and the extract from the confirmation service, page 92, in *The Alternative Service Book 1980*, are reproduced by permission of the Central Board of Finance of the Church of England.

Little-Born Jesus, page 21, first appeared in *Home and Family* 1963 and is quoted by Violet Madge in *Children in Search of Meaning*, SCM Press 1965.

Chrismons from Canada, page 25, and the extract from the Mothers' Union prayer, page 89, are reproduced by permission of the Mothers' Union.

Wise Men They Came, page 34, *This Joyful Eastertide*, page 54, and *Jesus the Lord of Love and Life*, page 86, are reproduced by permission of Jubilate Hymns. For USA: reproduced by permission of Hope Publishing Company.

Praise King Jesus, page 48, © 1970 Scripture Union, London, from *Come and Sing*. All rights reserved. used by permission.

Eric Milner-White: *My God, My Glory* (1954), page 76, extract reproduced by permission of SPCK, London.

Prayer for relaxing as a family, page 80, from *Prayers for all the Family* (1968), reproduced by permission of Epworth Press, London.

J.D.C Pellow, *Bread*, page 69, from *Here's the Year*, reproduced by permission of Julia Macrae Books.

Thanksgiving after Childbirth, page 81, from the *Book of Common Prayer 1662*, the rights of which are vested in the Crown in perpetuity within the United Kingdom, are reproduced by permission of Eyre & Spottiswoode Publishers, Her Majesty's Printers, London.

Scripture quotations from the Revised Standard Version of the Bible are copyrighted 1971 and 1952 by the Division of Christian Education of the National Council of the Churches of Christ in the USA.

Scripture quotations from The Holy Bible, New International Version. Copyright © 1973, 1978, 1974 by International Bible Society. Anglicisation © 1984 by Hodder & Stoughton Ltd. NIV Bible quotations used by permission of Hodder & Stoughton Ltd.

Scripture quotations from the Good News Bible (British usage edition), published by The Bible Societies and Collins, © American Bible Society 1966, 1971, 1976, are used by permission.

CONTENTS

INTRODUCTION

THE FESTIVALS

OTHER CELEBRATIONS

About the recipes

SPOON MEASUREMENTS

Standard spoon measurements are used
in all recipes
1 tablespoon – one 15ml spoon
1 teaspoon   – one 5ml spoon

All spoon measures are level.

QUANTITIES

For all recipes, quantities are given in metric,
imperial and American measures. Follow one set of
measures only; they are not interchangeable.

Where amounts of salt and pepper are not specified,
the cook should use his or her own discretion.

PASTRY

For basic pastry recipe see page 30 under
Black Bun.

INTRODUCTION

I suppose the first stirrings of this book started a long time ago when I was working with Jewish people. I was impressed by the integration of religious festivals with family home life. More than ever before, I believe that families today need encouragement to do things together in the home.

In today's mobile society family and cultural customs are being lost and with them I fear we are losing sight of the importance of doing things together. The modern world we live in gives us many advantages with instant this and frozen that; central heating and air conditioning keep us at a similar temperature all year round. But sadly this blurs the progress from one season to another and much of the annual pattern is slipping away.

The festivals of the Christian year give us a wonderful framework to take in a great variety of celebrations expressing different moods and emotions. I hope therefore that *Feasting for Festivals* will help us to do more together, to share that togetherness with our neighbours and to enjoy our God with each other in the home.

Jan Wilson

ADVENT AND CHRISTMAS

ADVENT AND CHRISTMAS

In those days Caesar Augustus issued a decree that a census should be taken of the entire Roman world. This was the first census that took place while Quirinius was governor of Syria. And everyone went to his own town to register. So Joseph went up from the town of Nazareth in Galilee to Judea, to Bethlehem the town of David, because he belonged to the house and line of David. He went there to register with Mary, who was pledged to be married to him and was expecting a child. While they were there the time came for the baby to be born, and she gave birth to her firstborn, a son. She wrapped him in cloths and placed him in a manger, because there was no room for them in the inn.

LUKE 2:1-7 New International Version

Christmas is probably the most widely celebrated festival in the world. People of different religions and no religion will send cards and give presents. Enemies will call a truce and even those engaged in active warfare will stop killing each other for the

Advent Crown

Making an Advent wreath or crown is a custom which originated in Germany and symbolizes the coming of Christ into a dark world. The wreaths consist of a circle of evergreen twigs with four candles standing in the ring. Sometimes they are hung from the ceiling and sometimes put in the centre of the dining table. The evergreen circle reminds us of God's never ending love and the candles of the light of Christ. On each of the Sundays in Advent a new candle is lit, so that by the Sunday before Christmas four candles are burning. Sometimes a fifth candle is added, usually larger than the others, and this is lit on Christmas Day. As the weeks go by and more candles are lit, the light gets brighter as we near the day when we remember Jesus Christ being born into our world. Here is a simple way to make an Advent wreath.

1 Fill a bowl with damp earth.

2 Decorate with holly, ivy, laurel or any available greenery.

3 Put four candles (white or red) into the earth.

4 Add ribbon. This can easily be done using florist's ribbon tied onto stab wires, also available from florists.

hours of Christmas Day. And all because a tiny baby was born two thousand years ago in a dirty stable in some obscure little village called Bethlehem.

In the four weeks before Christmas, which the Christian church calls *Advent* (it means 'coming'), Christians think of Jesus coming in three ways: as a baby; as a Saviour to any who will receive him; and as God in glory at the end of time.

Christmas is coming and the panic has begun.
Please look after mother, 'cause it isn't any fun
Shopping, cooking, cleaning, plus a thousand things to do
If you haven't brought a helping hand, Just keep well out of view!

Light a candle on each Sunday in Advent when all the family are gathered. This could be at the main meal or the beginning or end of the day. Take turns to light the candle and perhaps use these words as the candles are lit. The person lighting each candle says: 'Come Lord Jesus.' And all reply: 'And bring love' (week 1); 'And bring hope' (week 2); 'And bring peace' (week 3); 'And bring joy' (week 4).

If there is a candle for Christmas Day, the person lighting the candle says: 'Jesus Christ is born today.'

All reply: 'Glory to God in the highest.'

Honigkuchen

HONEY CAKE Germany

CAKE:

½ tbsp	½ tbsp	½ tbsp	soft butter
1¼ lb	575 g	5 cups	plain flour
1½ tsp	1½ tsp	1½ tsp	baking powder
3 oz	75 g	¾ cup	ground almonds
2½ tbsp	2½ tbsp	2½ tbsp	finely chopped candied lemon peel
2½ tbsp	2½ tbsp	2½ tbsp	cocoa
1 tsp	1 tsp	1 tsp	ground cloves
1 tsp	1 tsp	1 tsp	cinnamon
1½ tsp	1½ tsp	1½ tsp	ground cardamom
1 tsp	1 tsp	1 tsp	grated lemon rind
½ tsp	½ tsp	½ tsp	almond essence (extract)
¾ lb	325 g	1 cup	honey
½ lb	225 g	1 cup	sugar
6 tbsp	6 tbsp	6 tbsp	cold water

ALMOND GLAZE:

4 oz	125 g	1 cup	icing (confectioners) sugar
½ tsp	½ tsp	½ tsp	almond essence (extract)
1 tsp	1 tsp	1 tsp	lemon juice
5 tbsp	5 tbsp	5 tbsp	cold water

METHOD

1 Grease and flour a Swiss roll tin (Bundt pan).

2 Put honey, sugar and cold water into a pan. Heat slowly until the sugar has dissolved. Bring to the boil and then simmer for 5 minutes.

3 Stir all other cake ingredients together in a bowl.

4 Pour on the honey and sugar solution and mix to a smooth dough.

5 Put into the prepared tin and spread evenly.

6 Bake in oven Gas Mark 4/180°C/350°F for 20 minutes. The cake should be firm to the touch.

7 Prepare glaze by bringing the ingredients slowly to the boil, stirring continuously. Then simmer for 3 minutes.

8 Remove the cake from the tin. Place on a cooling tray and pour the glaze over it.

9 When cold, store in an airtight tin for several days to allow the cake to mellow.

An Advent calendar

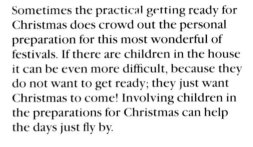

Advent calendars were first produced in Germany in 1890 but can now be found almost anywhere. They have one window to be opened for each day, from the first day in December to Christmas Eve. Inside each window is a picture of something having to do with Christmas: an angel, a star, and so on. Making your own Advent calendar with a large piece of paper and pictures cut from old Christmas cards can be fun. Here's another more original idea, using matchboxes.

1 Glue twenty-four matchboxes together, as shown.

2 Cover the top and sides with Christmas paper.

3 Number each box either in order or jumbled up.

4 Put a sweet (candy), a tiny toy or a Christmas picture in each box.

5 Open one box each day.

Sometimes the practical getting ready for Christmas does crowd out the personal preparation for this most wonderful of festivals. If there are children in the house it can be even more difficult, because they do not want to get ready; they just want Christmas to come! Involving children in the preparations for Christmas can help the days just fly by.

St Nicholas

It is difficult to separate fact from legend in a story as old as that of St Nicholas. We do know that he was bishop of Myra on the south coast of Turkey in the fourth century. He was imprisoned for his faith and some say martyred during the reign of Diocletian, the Roman Emperor. He was always kind to young people and became the patron saint of children, merchants and sailors, as well as of Russia. The best-known story about St Nicholas tells how he provided money for dowries for three poor sisters so that they might be happily married. It is believed he died on 6 December in AD 326 and this day is commemorated each year in many countries.

In Germany, Holland, Switzerland and France St Nicholas visits children on his day. In some countries he is known by his nickname 'Santa Claus'. In Germany he appears in schools and will throw sweets or biscuits (cookies) called *pernoten* for the children to gather. The festival of St Nicholas is seen as a community celebration, whereas Christmas is a family time. St Nicholas, dressed in bishop's robes, asks the children questions about the Christmas story and whether they have been good or bad throughout the year. His companion, Black Peter, writes down the names of any children not knowing the right answers or who have been naughty. They are then urged to put the matter right before Christmas.

In Holland St Nicholas and Black Peter arrive by steamer at the port of Amsterdam. St Nicholas rides a white horse and, followed by a procession of excited children, visits the town and gives presents to the children. In Dutch homes on St

Speculatius

Denmark

3 oz	75 g	6 tbsp	butter or margarine
6 oz	175 g	1½ cups	plain flour
1	1	1	small egg
3 oz	75 g	⅓ cup	brown sugar
pinch	pinch	pinch	cloves and cardamom
1 tsp	1 tsp	1 tsp	cinnamon

METHOD

1 Rub the butter into the flour.

2 Cream the egg with the sugar, and add to the flour and butter mixture.

3 Add the spices and mix together gently.

4 Cut into shapes and put on to a greased baking tray.

5 Bake in oven at Gas Mark 4/180°C/350°F for 10 minutes or until golden brown.

6 Cool and store in an airtight container. The biscuits will keep for several weeks.

Haselnussmakronen

HAZELNUT MACAROONS Germany

6 oz	175 g	¾ cup	sugar
7½ oz	215 g	1 cup	ground hazelnuts (filberts) or almonds
1½ tbsp	1½ tbsp	1½ tbsp	cocoa
2 tsp	2 tsp	2 tsp	grated lemon rind
½ tsp	½ tsp	½ tsp	vanilla essence (extract)
2	2	2	egg whites
			pinch of salt

METHOD

1 Whisk egg whites until stiff.

2 Add the sugar and continue whisking until the mixture stands in stiff peaks.

3 Add the remaining ingredients and fold in gently.

4 Drop teaspoonfuls of mixture on to a greased baking tray at least 1 in./2.5 cm apart. Allow to stand.

5 Bake in oven at Gas Mark 2/150°C/300°F for ½ hour. Carefully transfer to a cooling tray and store in an airtight container. They will keep for several weeks.

Springerle

Germany

1 oz	25 g	2 tbsp	melted butter
3 oz	75 g	3/4 cup	aniseed
2	2	2	eggs
10 oz	275 g	1¼ cups	sugar
1 tsp	1 tsp	1 tsp	lemon rind
½ tsp	½ tsp	½ tsp	vanilla essence (extract)
12 oz	350 g	3 cups	plain flour

METHOD

1 Grease baking trays with melted butter and sprinkle with aniseed.

2 Beat the eggs until they begin to thicken.

3 Add to the sugar and whisk until thick.

4 Beat in the lemon rind and vanilla essence (extract).

5 Add the flour one-third at a time until the mixture forms a soft ball.

6 Knead for 10 minutes.

7 Roll out until ¼ in./0.6 cm thick.

8 Cut into shapes as required and put on to the prepared baking trays.

9 Set aside for 24 hours.

10 Bake in oven at Gas Mark ½/130°C/250°F for 20-30 minutes or until firm but not brown.

11 Cool and leave uncovered for 2-3 days to soften. Then store in an airtight container. They will keep for several weeks.

Nicholas' Eve the children wait with mounting excitement for the doorbell to ring. This is the signal for them to rush to the door to find the basket of presents which he has left on the step. In France St Nicholas travels by donkey and the children leave hay beside the fireplace as a treat for the animal. St Nicholas' favourite drink, and therefore always part of the celebrations, is hot chocolate. In Germany he is given honey cake (see page 13) and in Holland they bake a marvellous St Nicholas' cake of puff pastry filled with marzipan and nuts (see page 17). In the places where St Nicholas calls there is always a large tray of assorted biscuits (cookies) ready for him and any other visitors that might call during the Advent season.

Christmas food preparation

The Sunday before Advent is often referred to as 'Stir-up' Sunday, and ladies in church in England may be heard to ask each other, 'Have you made your puddings yet?' or 'Is your cake baked yet?' The expression 'Stir-up' comes from words in the special prayer for that day in the Church of England Prayer Book.

Stir up, O Lord,
the wills of your faithful people;
that richly bearing the fruit of good
works,
they may by you be richly rewarded;
through Jesus Christ our Lord.

Collect for the fifth Sunday before Christmas from *The Alternative Service Book.*

As we pray those words it is hard for any keen cook to keep her mind from wandering to the many preparations to be made for the fast approaching festival. In most traditions there are things which can be done in advance to ease the busyness at Christmas.

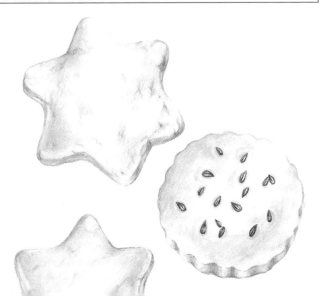

The Christmas tree

As with many legends, there are several stories about the origin of the Christmas tree. One tells of St Boniface, who went from England to Germany to spread the Christian message. One frosty night in December he came across a group of people about to sacrifice a little boy to their god Odin. The boy was tied to an oak tree and Boniface untied him and chopped down the tree. Then they saw a little fir tree growing between the roots of the oak. Boniface told the people then and there about Jesus and how he had come to bring light to a dark world. The people listening stepped forward in response and hung their lanterns on the fir tree as a symbol of Jesus, their new light.

Another story tells how Martin Luther, the great church reformer, was walking through the woods one night. He was struck by the number of stars in the sky. He brought home a fir tree and set candles on it, telling his children it was to remind them of Jesus who left the glory of heaven to come to earth.

Whether or not there is any truth in these legends, the Christmas tree seems to have originated in Germany. The custom was probably taken to the United States of America in 1776 by soldiers fighting in the American War of Independence, and to Britain by Queen Victoria's husband, Prince Albert.

The custom has spread to many countries — and if there are no fir trees, other trees will do! In Madagascar a mango or eucalyptus tree is used and decorated with cotton-wool snow, while in South Africa a tree in the garden is decorated as a Christmas tree. In New Zealand the lovely blossoming tree *Pohutukawa* is called the Christmas tree because its beautiful red flowers bloom in December. In Denmark Christmas trees are decorated with red and white paper roses and criss-cross hearts. On 6 January in Germany the children are allowed to raid the Christmas tree and eat any goodies left on it; in Sweden the children have a special Plundering Party.

Children can help decorate the Christmas tree, and some home-made

Letterbanket

ST NICHOLAS' CAKE Holland

14 oz	400 g	14 oz	puff pastry
8 oz	200 g	8 oz	marzipan (almond paste)
4 oz	100 g	1 cup	icing (confectioners) sugar
			juice of a lemon
			a few nuts and cherries, chopped

METHOD

1 Roll out the pastry to form a large rectangle and cut into strips about 12 in × 2 in./30 cm × 5 cm.

2 Roll the marzipan into long 'sausages' (the thickness of a finger) about 12 in./30 cm long.

3 Lay the marzipan sausages on to the pastry strips. Dampen the edges of the pastry and roll around the marzipan.

4 Cut into pieces about 4 in./10 cm long and mould into initials or letters to form the words 'St Nicholas' or any other words of your choice.

5 Put on to a greased baking tray and allow to stand for 30 minutes.

6 Bake in oven at Gas Mark 7/210°C/425°F for 10-15 minutes.

7 Transfer on to a cooling tray.

8 Make icing with the icing sugar and lemon juice, and ice the letters. Decorate with nuts and cherries.

Peppernoten

PEPPER NUTS Holland

8 oz	225 g	2 cups	plain flour
6 oz	175 g	¾ cup	margarine or butter
6 oz	175 g	¾ cup	dark brown sugar
1 tsp	1 tsp	1 tsp	baking powder
2 tsp	2 tsp	2 tsp	mixed spice (pumpkin pie spice)
2 tsp	2 tsp	2 tsp	cinnamon
1 dstsp	1 dstsp	1 tbsp	milk
			grated rind of 1 lemon
			pinch of salt

METHOD

1 Beat sugar, butter, lemon rind and salt together in a bowl until soft and creamy.

2 Add the milk and then all other ingredients to form a stiff dough.

3 Roll marble-sized pieces into balls and put on to a greased baking tray.

4 Bake in oven at Gas Mark 4/180°C/350°F for 15 minutes. Allow to cool.

5 Store in an airtight tin or jar. The peppernoten will keep for several weeks and need to be eaten by the handful!

sweets and cookies (see pages 26-27) always add to the attraction of the tree. Little stockings, made out of odd scraps of material, can be filled with a striped candy bar or a few home-made sweets. These not only look attractive, but can be a treat for visiting children.

The Christmas crib

This ought to take pride of place among the Christmas decorations as it tells the story of Jesus' birth in the stable, and how shepherds visited him. Many years ago, in the thirteenth century, when most ordinary people could not read, St Francis decided he would demonstrate the Christmas story in a way anyone could understand. He set up a stable scene in a cave not far from his home in Assisi, with real people and animals. As people gathered around to see what he was doing, he told them how Jesus had been born in a simple stable and how angels had appeared to shepherds telling them to go and find for themselves the Messiah who had been born. The idea gradually caught on and now the Christmas Crib (also called a creche or Nativity scene) is a universal part of the celebrations.

When St Francis set up the first Christmas Crib he wanted to convey the wonder and excitement of how God came to us as a tiny baby. We can still convey that wonder to our children. For example, we

A snowman decoration

1 Cover a toilet roll tube with cotton wool.

2 Make the snowman's head by rolling some cotton wool into a ball. Place this on top of the tube. Carefully draw his eyes, nose and mouth with a black felt-tip pen.

3 The tree is made by placing a twig in a decorated yoghurt pot filled with earth. You can then tie small sweets on the tree.

4 Place the snowman and the tree on a piece of thick card covered with cotton wool.

can leave the figure of baby Jesus to be put into the manger first thing on Christmas morning.

There are many ways of making a crib. Have you tried dressing up *Playpeople* or other toy figures using coloured paper or pieces of material? It is easier than making your own figures.

In France the crib has additional figures of local craftsmen — bakers, carpenters, and so on — to symbolize everyone coming to the stable to worship Jesus.

Christmas customs from around the world

In many parts of the world the main family celebration is on Christmas Eve. In Poland, the Ukraine, Sweden, Denmark, Germany and Austria the main present giving and feasting is done then. In Poland and the Ukraine children watch excitedly for the first star to appear in the sky, for that is the sign for the festivities to begin.

In Poland the main item in the feast is the carp, a freshwater fish. Wherever in the world she happens to be, a Polish woman

Stollen

Germany

In Germany *Stollen* is made in advance for eating at Christmas and giving as gifts.

2 tsp	2 tsp	2 tsp	dried yeast
1 tbsp	1 tbsp	1 tbsp	lukewarm water
4 fl oz	175 ml	¾ cup	lukewarm milk
4 oz	125 g	1 stick	butter
1 lb	500 g	4 cups	flour
1 tsp	1 tsp	1 tsp	salt
½ tsp	½ tsp	½ tsp	ground cinnamon
¼ tsp	¼ tsp	¼ tsp	ground mace
¼ tsp	¼ tsp	¼ tsp	ground cardamom
6 oz	185 g	¾ cup	sugar
2	2	2	eggs, lightly beaten
6 oz	175 g	1 cup	candied peel, chopped
3 oz	75 g	½ cup	sultanas (golden raisins)
2½ oz	65 g	½ cup	walnuts, chopped

ICING:

1 oz	25 g	1 tbsp	butter
8 oz	250 g	2 cups	icing (confectioners) sugar
2 tbsp	2 tbsp	2 tbsp	water
¼ tsp	¼ tsp	¼ tsp	vanilla essence (extract)
			walnut halves

METHOD

1 Add the warm water to half the warm milk and sprinkle the dried yeast on top. Allow to stand for 10-15 minutes, until frothy.

2 Mix all the dry ingredients together in a large bowl.

3 Add the eggs and half the butter to the remaining milk and mix together with the frothy yeast.

4 Add the liquid to the dry ingredients to make a soft dough.

5 Knead the dough on a floured board for 10 minutes. Put dough back into bowl, cover and allow to rise until doubled in bulk.

6 Divide the dough in two and roll out each portion to form a large oval. Brush each with melted butter and roll up.

7 Place on greased baking tins, cover and allow to rise until doubled in size.

8 Bake in oven at Gas Mark 5/190°C/375°F for 30-35 minutes. Allow to cool.

9 When *Stollen* are cool make up the icing by melting the butter and stirring in the other icing ingredients. Spread on top and sides of *Stollen* and decorate with walnut halves.

Saffronsbrod

SAFFRON BREAD Sweden

2 tsp	2 tsp	2 tsp	sugar
¼ pint	125 ml	½ cup	warm water
1 tsp	1 tsp	1 tsp	saffron powder
2 lb	1 kg	8 cups	strong plain flour (all purpose flour)
4 tsp	4 tsp	4 tsp	salt
4 oz	100 g	½ cup	butter
6 oz	150 g	¾ cup	castor (table) sugar
2 oz	50 g	¼ cup	raisins
1 tsp	1 tsp	1 tsp	ground cardamom
¾ pint	375 ml	1½ cups	lukewarm milk
			beaten egg for brushing

TOPPING:

1 tbsp	1 tbsp	1 tbsp	chopped almonds
1 tbsp	1 tbsp	1 tbsp	coarsely crushed cube sugar

METHOD

1 Dissolve sugar in the warm water and add yeast.

2 Mix the saffron powder with 1 tbsp hot water.

3 Leave about 20 minutes, until frothy.

4 Sift flour and salt and rub in the butter. Add castor sugar, cardamom and raisins.

5 Mix to a dough with the yeast mixture and milk and add saffron.

6 Knead thoroughly, return to bowl, cover and allow to rise until doubled in bulk.

7 Shape into small buns, put on a greased baking tray until doubled in size. Brush with beaten egg, sprinkle with coarse sugar and almonds.

8 Bake in oven at Gas Mark 6/200°C/400°F for 10-15 minutes or until golden brown.

9 Cool on a cooling tray.

10 Serve fresh with coffee.

St Lucy's day

On 13 December people in Sweden celebrate St Lucy's Day. They remember how Lucia, a young girl, brought food to persecuted Christians hiding in the catacombs in Rome during the time of Emperor Diocletian. In order that she could carry the food and see where she was going in the dark, Lucia wore candles on her head. On St Lucy's Day each year by tradition one of the daughters of the family is chosen to be St Lucy. She gets up early and takes coffee and 'Lucia' buns (*Saffronsbrod*) to the rest of the family who are still in bed. She dresses in a white robe with a scarlet sash and wears on her head a crown of green leaves with five candles in it. Sometimes she is escorted by boys dressed in long white shirts and pointed hats, called star boys.

will try to get a carp to cook. But before anything else is eaten the head of the household breaks a special Christmas wafer called *Oplatek*. This is specially made with a picture of the Nativity on it. The wafer is broken and a piece passed to each member of the family in turn. As they receive the wafer they hug and kiss one another and offer Christmas greetings. A space is always set for Jesus or a passing stranger who would be welcomed to join the meal.

In Sweden boiled ham is served at midday on Christmas Eve, together with herring and beetroot salad, meatballs and beans. In the evening *Risgrynsgrot*, a thick rice porridge sprinkled with cinnamon, is eaten.

In Norway many different kinds of biscuits (cookies) are baked in preparation for Christmas. A sudden thaw which comes in December after the first winter snow is called a 'biscuit thaw' and attributed to the overworked ovens!

French families return from church on Christmas Eve to a meal known as *Le Reveillon*, which may be roast fowl or baked ham with salad followed by cake and fruit. A favourite cake is Chestnut Yule Log.

In Germany, too, the festivities begin on Christmas Eve. The children eagerly wait outside the best room in the house, which has been kept locked all of Christmas Eve. But they are allowed to look through the keyhole and when they see the candles on the tree have been lit they know that the *Christkindchen* or Christ Child has been with the presents.

Then the door is opened and they go in to receive their gifts. This is followed by a hot drink with special biscuits (cookies) and then it is time for bed. Each child leaves a special Christmas plate out on the window-sill or beside the bed. In the morning this is full of sweets, nuts, biscuits and fruit which are the child's treat to eat over the Christmas holiday.

Similarly, in Austria on Christmas Eve the family congregate outside the closed door of the sitting-room. The children listen for the *Christkindchen* to ring a bell signalling that the presents have been

Little-Born Jesus

(Sung by Lucy, aged four, to her doll and noted down by her mother.)

When the baby borned
Joseph said to Mary
'What am I going to do about
This little-born Jesus baby Christ?
I never knew it was going to be like this
With all these angels and kings
And shepherds and stars and things.
It's got me all worried, I can tell you
On Christmas Day in the morning.'

Mary said to Joseph,
'Not to worry my darling,
Dear old darling Joseph.
Everything's going to be all right,
Because the angel told me not to fear;
So just hold up the lamp
So I can see the dear, funny, sweet little
  face
Of my darling little-born Jesus baby
  Christ.'

Joseph said to Mary,
'Behold the handyman of the Lord.'

Happy Christmas, Happy Christmas,
Christ is born today.

delivered and all is ready. The family go in to find a Christmas tree ablaze with candles and, in pride of place, the Crib surrounded by gifts.

Christmas is celebrated on 6 January in Russia. Many Christians fast throughout Advent so Christmas is a time for great feasting. Traditionally a meal of twelve courses was served in honour of the twelve Apostles.

In Holland Christmas is a quieter family affair after the celebrations of St Nicholas. The day begins with a breakfast of bread with cold meats and cheeses followed by the popular *Kerst Krans* or Christmas ring. This is similar to St Nicholas' cake, but is shaped into a ring. The main meal in the evening will consist

Christmas Cake

England

2 lb	900 g	4 cups	mixed dried fruit
3 oz	75 g	3/4 cup	glacé (maraschino) cherries, halved
3 oz	75 g	3/4 cup	chopped almonds
			grated rind of one lemon
2 1/2 tbsp	2 1/2 tbsp	2 1/2 tbsp	brandy (optional)
9 oz	250 g	2 1/4 cups	plain flour
1 1/4 tsp	1 1/4 tsp	1 1/4 tsp	mixed spice
1/2 tsp	1/2 tsp	1/2 tsp	grated nutmeg
3 oz	75 g	3/4 cup	ground almonds
8 oz	225 g	1 cup	butter or margarine
8 oz	225 g	1 cup	soft brown sugar
1 tbsp	1 tbsp	1 tbsp	black treacle (dark molasses)
5	5	5	eggs

METHOD

1 Prepare a tin (9 in. round or 8 in. square) by lining it with greaseproof paper or baking parchment.

2 Cream butter and sugar together.

3 Add eggs one at a time with a spoonful of flour until all have been added. Beat in the treacle or molasses.

4 Fold in the remaining flour with the spices and ground nuts.

5 Fold in fruit, nuts, cherries and stir in the brandy if being used.

6 Put the mixture into the prepared tin and level the surface of the mixture.

7 Protect the sides of the cake from burning with a double layer of brown paper tied round with string.

8 Bake at Gas Mark 1/140°C/275°F for 3 1/2-4 1/2 hours or until a fork pushed to the bottom comes out clean.

9 Allow to cool and store in an airtight tin until required. About ten days before Christmas cover the top and sides of the cake with almond paste. Leave in a cool dry place. When the almond paste is dry, ice with royal or fondant icing.

Fondant Icing

1 lb	450 g	4 cups	icing (confectioners) sugar
1	1	1	egg white
1 1/2 tbsp	1 1/2 tbsp	1 1/2 tbsp	liquid glucose, warmed

METHOD

1 Blend all the ingredients together with a knife.

2 Knead very thoroughly on a board dusted with a little icing sugar to prevent it sticking.

3 Roll out the icing with a rolling pin until large enough to cover the top and sides of the cake.

4 Brush the cake with a little egg white and lift the fondant icing carefully over.

5 Trim the bottom edges with a knife and decorate as required.

Royal Icing

1½ lb	700 g	6 cups	icing (confectioners) sugar, sifted
3	3	3	egg whites
			few drops of lemon juice

1 tsp glycerine can be added (if available) to prevent the icing hardening too much, but this is not essential.

METHOD

1 Put egg whites into a bowl and beat lightly with an electric mixer or a wooden spoon.

2 Add the sifted sugar gradually, beating it in well.

3 Add sufficient sugar to make a mixture that will hold its shape when spread.

4 Beat in the lemon juice and glycerine if used.

5 Cover with a damp cloth and allow to stand for one hour.

6 Cover the top and sides of the cake as required.

of game or fowl served with a fruit compôte, red cabbage, potatoes and peas. A light blancmange served with cream will usually follow.

In England, apart from the short period in the seventeenth century when the Puritans ordered fasting not feasting for Christmas, food has always played an important part in the celebrations. The Italians have a saying for a busy person that 'he has more to do than the ovens in England at Christmas'. In Cornwall there is a saying that 'the devil himself dare not appear in Cornwall during Christmas for fear of being baked in a pie'.

For many years the boar's head was the main item of Christmas dinner, followed by peacock or swan. Since the middle of the sixteenth century, when the first turkeys were brought over from America, turkey has been the most popular dish. It is said that King George II reared three thousand turkeys in Richmond Park near London to feed to his guests at Christmas time. Christmas pudding or plum pudding has long been the traditional sweet which follows. Mincemeat pies, so named because they did once contain minced lamb, remain a favourite. Mince pies were once oval in shape to represent the manger in which Jesus slept. This probably changed during the Puritan era when people disguised their Christmas mince pies as ordinary pasties. In England Father Christmas (a jolly old gentleman with lots of white hair and whiskers who wears a red suit) brings gifts for the children. He arrives during the night of Christmas Eve

Christmas Pudding

England

If you have never made a Christmas pudding before, make it with a friend and split the mixture. There is enough in this recipe for two medium puddings. Doing it together is fun and gives confidence.

4 oz	125 g	1 cup	flour
2 oz	50 g	¾ cup	breadcrumbs
1 tsp	1 tsp	1 tsp	mixed spice (pumpkin spice)
1 tsp	1 tsp	1 tsp	cinnamon
1 tsp	1 tsp	1 tsp	nutmeg
4 oz	125 g	¾ cup	shredded suet
4 oz	125 g	2 cups	brown sugar
4 oz	125 g	1 cup	grated apple
1	1	1	small grated carrot
2	2	2	eggs
1¼ lb	575 g	3 cups	mixed dried fruit
3 oz	75 g	½ cup	chopped prunes
4 oz	125 g	1 cup	chopped almonds
½	½	½	grated lemon rind
½	½	½	juice lemon
½	½	½	grated orange rind
1 tbsp	1 tbsp	1 tbsp	black treacle (dark molasses)
¼ pint	150 ml	½ cup	milk or ale

METHOD

1 Mix all the dry ingredients together in a large bowl.

2 Stir in all other ingredients, mix well and allow to stand – overnight if possible.

3 Put mixture into one large or two smaller pudding bowls, and cover with greaseproof paper and foil or a pudding cloth.

4 Steam for 6-8 hours.

5 Remove damp coverings and replace with new ones.

6 Store until required and steam for a further 2 hours on Christmas Day. Serve with custard or brandy butter and cream.

and leaves presents in stockings hung up on the mantelpiece or at the end of the bed.

In Ireland on Christmas Eve the youngest child lights a candle in the window as a sign of welcome to the holy family seeking shelter.

America has a rich variety of Christmas traditions. Santa Claus is the bringer of gifts. Like Father Christmas he travels through the sky in a sleigh pulled by reindeer. He comes down the chimney and leaves presents in stockings.

In some parts of America there are beautiful outdoor Nativity scenes called Christmas Gardens. Also popular is the 'flower of the holy night', the poinsettia, representing the star of Bethlehem and

What are Christingles?

Christingle means Christ-Light. Christingle services take place in many churches at Christmas to celebrate the coming of Christ, the light, into the world. The ceremony is very old, though no one knows just how far back it goes. However, in recent years the service has been revived in Britain by the Church of England Children's Society. At the services children (and adults) exchange a gift of money for a Christingle. The money raised is given to families in need.

How to make a Christingle

1 Make a hole in the top of an orange. Do not make the hole too large. Place a candle in the hole.

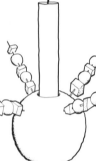

named after Joel R Poinsett, Ambassador to Mexico, who brought the poinsettia to the United States in 1829.

Canadians decorate the Christmas tree with 'Chrismons'. A Chrismon gets its name from a combination of two words: Christ and Monogram. The monograms are all symbols which relate in some way to Jesus Christ. Many of them were used by the first Christians to identify themselves to one another — a star, a fish, a lamb, a cross. They are made in colour combinations of white, gold and silver which symbolize the purity and majesty of the Son of God. The evergreen tree they hang on is a reminder of the eternal life which Jesus promises. Chrismons are made out of card or polystyrene, and decorated with paint, beads or glitter.

In India a star is used to show that a particular house belongs to Christians and the occupants are celebrating Christmas. The star is normally about four feet high and made of bamboo sticks covered on all sides with white paper. It is usually hung outside the house with a light to show it off. *Kal-Kal* is rather like a small doughnut and is cooked at Christmas to offer to visitors who drop in.

In Australia a flower called the Christmas Bell blooms at Christmas. It has a bell-shaped yellow flower surrounded by bright green leaves and it makes a lovely decoration. For Australians, Christmas comes at the beginning of the long summer holidays, so it is extra exciting for the

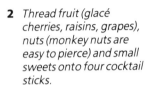

2 Thread fruit (glacé cherries, raisins, grapes), nuts (monkey nuts are easy to pierce) and small sweets onto four cocktail sticks.

3 Push the cocktail sticks into the orange to surround the candle.

4 Tie a piece of red ribbon (or flame-proof crêpe paper) around the middle of the orange.

5 Cut a square of aluminium foil (at least 25 cm square) and place the orange in the centre. Fold the foil up around the fruit so that it forms a shield to catch any dripping wax.

What do the different parts of a Christingle represent?

The orange represents the world. The candle represents the light that Jesus brings to the world. The red band represents the blood Christ shed for us. The four cocktail sticks represent the four seasons. The nuts and fruit represent the fruits of the earth.

A Christmas quiz

The answers are all to be found in the Bible in Matthew's Gospel chapters 1 and 2. Or in Luke's Gospel chapter 1 and chapter 2 verses 1 to 40.

1 In Matthew's Gospel how many generations are recorded between Abraham and the Messiah?

2 How many gifts did the Wise Men bring to Jesus?

3 In the accounts of Jesus' birth how many visits from angels are there?

4 How many months did Mary stay with her cousin Elizabeth while they were both pregnant?

5 How old was Anna the prophetess?

6 How many months had Elizabeth been pregnant when the angel appeared to Mary?

7 How many different names are given to Jesus in these passages?

8 How many times do angels say 'Do not be afraid'?

9 How many prophecies are quoted from the Old Testament in the Matthew passages?

10 How many days old was Jesus when he was circumcised and given his name?

(Answers on page 92)

CANDY-MAKING

Sweets and candies packaged nicely make delightful presents. With a little supervision children can make these.

Fruit and Nut Clusters

England

3 oz	75 g	¾ cup	toasted hazelnuts (or almonds)
2 oz	50 g	½ cup	walnuts
2 oz	50 g	½ cup	glacé (candied) cherries
7 oz	200 g	7 squares	chocolate

METHOD

1 Roughly chop the nuts and cherries.
2 Melt the chocolate in a bowl over hot water.
3 Stir the nuts and cherries into the chocolate.
4 Drop a teaspoonful of the mixture into paper sweet cases (or candy cups) and leave in a cool place to set.

Gum Nut Chews

Australia

4 oz	125 g	½ cup	dried fruit
½ oz	15 g	1 tbsp	glacé (candied) cherries
8 oz	225 g	3 cup	cornflakes
4 oz	125 g	1½ cup	coconut, shredded
½ tsp	½ tsp	½ tsp	vanilla essence (extract)
½ pint	300 ml	1 cup	condensed milk

chocolate vermicelli, drinking chocolate, or powdered hot chocolate mix

METHOD

1 Chop the dried fruit and the cherries.
2 Crush the cornflakes and add to fruit, coconut and vanilla.
3 Add sufficient condensed milk to bind the mixture together. Take care not to let it get too wet.
4 Roll teaspoon-size pieces into balls and roll in powdered chocolate.
5 Place on a plate or in paper sweet cases (paper candy cups) and leave overnight to set.

Peppermint Creams

England

1 lb	450 g	4 cups	icing (confectioners) sugar
1	1	1	egg
½	½	½	lemon
½ tsp	½ tsp	½ tsp	peppermint essence (extract)

METHOD

1 Sift the icing sugar into a bowl.
2 Separate the egg. The best way of doing this is to break the egg into a saucer, put an egg cup over the yolk, and pour off the white holding on to the egg cup carefully.
3 Mix the egg white into the icing sugar. If the mixture is too stiff to hold together, squeeze the juice from the lemon and add a little, drop by drop, until the mixture is firm but smooth.
4 Add the peppermint essence.
5 Roll out on a surface dusted with icing sugar and cut into shapes. Leave in a cool place to set.

If you wish to make different flavoured creams you could divide the mixture before adding the peppermint. Then add peppermint to one half and coffee, almond essence or grated orange rind to the other half. Then continue as above.

Christmas Tree Cookie
Decorations

If you want edible decorations then follow the recipe for *Speculatius* (see page 15), but before baking make a hole through the cookie for hanging purposes. When they are cool you can colour the cookies with food colouring mixed with egg white. This mixture gives a nice shiny surface and can be painted on with a paint brush. Finally hang the decorations on the tree with ribbon.

If you want decorations that will last but are *not* to be eaten, then make them in the following way:

4 oz	125 g	1 cup	plain flour
1 tbsp	1 tbsp	1 tbsp	salt
¼ pint	150 ml	½ cup	cold water

METHOD

1 Mix the ingredients into a firm dough.

2 Roll out on a floured surface and cut into shapes as required. Make a hole through each before baking.

3 Bake in oven Gas Mark ½/130°C/250°F for 40 minutes.

4 Colour with poster paint or felt-tip pens and, when dry, varnish. Then hang on the tree with coloured ribbons.

A table decoration

1 The Father Christmas is made out of a toilet roll tube covered with red paper or cloth.

2 Make the head by forming a ball of tissue paper and draw on eyes, nose and mouth with a black felt-tip pen. Use a small amount of glue to attach this to the body.

3 Use cotton wool (cotton balls) for Father Christmas' hair and for the fur trim on his hood and sleeves.

4 Make the sack by sewing together two pieces of material. Then fill with small sweets, candies, or nuts and raisins.

5 Stand Father Christmas and his sack on a board covered with cotton wool.

YULE LOGS

Ginger Log

Australia

1 packet		10-20	ginger biscuits (ginger snaps)
¼ pint	150 ml	½ cup	whipping or double cream
			crystallized ginger

METHOD

1 Whip the cream until stiff.

2 Sandwich the biscuits with the cream and put on to a plate in a log shape.

3 Spread the remaining cream over the log and decorate with the crystallized ginger.

Bûche de Noël aux Marrons

CHESTNUT YULE LOG France

2 lb	1 kg	4 cups	unsweetened chestnut purée
4 oz	100 g	4 squares	plain chocolate (semi-sweet baking chocolate)
1 tbsp	1 tbsp	1 tbsp	strong black coffee
5 oz	125 g	¾ cup	softened butter
5 oz	125 g	1¼ cups	icing (confectioners) sugar

DECORATION:

Sifted icing or confectioners sugar and Christmas cake decorations.

METHOD

1 Beat the chestnut purée until smooth.

2 Melt the chocolate in a bowl over hot water and add the coffee.

3 Beat the butter and sugar with the chestnut and chocolate until smooth.

4 Chill in refrigerator for ½ hour.

5 Neatly shape the mixture into a log and mark it to look like bark.

6 Chill overnight. Then dust with icing sugar and decorate.

This is a very rich cake. As an alternative you could use a chocolate Swiss roll (or chocolate torte) as a base and mix up ¼ of the chestnut mixture to use as a covering.

children. As the weather is hot some families celebrate Christmas on the beach with cold turkey and salad. Others will eat hot turkey first and then visit the beach to cool off! Father Christmas visits the children and is sometimes pictured in a cart drawn by six white kangaroos. Ginger Log is a particular favourite Christmas dessert .

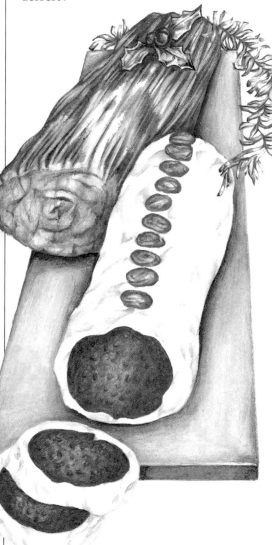

NEW YEAR

NEW YEAR

New Year festivals have been celebrated for more than five thousand years, some of them religious and some not. Several of the major world religions count New Year as a main celebration but the Christian church never really has. The Jews celebrate their new year as *Rosh Hashana* in September or October, and the Chinese have a Spring Festival which is a great occasion and an opportunity to make a fresh start.

The fixing of New Year's Day has had quite a chequered history in the western world and has at different times been on 1 March; 25 March; 25 December; and 1 January. The Gregorian Calendar established in 1582 set 1 January as New Year's Day and this was immediately adopted by Roman Catholic countries.

Black Bun
Scotland

BASIC PASTRY RECIPE:

8 oz	225 g	2 cups	flour
4 oz	115 g	½ cup	cooking fat (shortening)
			Water to mix
			Egg to glaze

FILLING:

1 lb	450 g	2 cups	currants (optional)
1 lb	450 g	2 cups	raisins
2 oz	50 g	¼ cup	candied peel
4 oz	100 g	½ cup	chopped almonds
4 oz	100 g	1 cup	flour
4 oz	100 g	½ cup	soft brown sugar
1 tsp	1 tsp	1 tsp	cinnamon or mixed spice (pumpkin spice)
1 tsp	1 tsp	1 tsp	nutmeg or mixed spice (pumpkin spice)
1 tsp	1 tsp	1 tsp	ginger or mixed spice (pumpkin spice)
1 tsp	1 tsp	1 tsp	ground cloves or mixed spice (pumpkin spice)
1 tsp	1 tsp	1 tsp	bicarbonate of soda (baking soda)
1 tsp	1 tsp	1 tsp	cream of tartar
1	1	1	egg
3 tbsp	3 tbsp	3 tbsp	black treacle (dark molasses)
8 tbsp	8 tbsp	8 tbsp	milk (or whisky)

METHOD

1. Make the pastry by rubbing the fat (shortening) in the flour, and mixing to a soft dough with cold water.

2. Roll out two-thirds of the pastry to make a circle about 14 in./35 cm across.

3. Grease an 8 in./20 cm round cake tin and line it with the pastry.

FILLING

4. Mix all the dry ingredients together in a large bowl.

5. Mix the egg, treacle (molasses) and milk together and stir into the dry mixture.

6. Turn this all into the pastry case.

7. Roll out the remaining pastry and put it on top of the filling.

8. Moisten the edges of the pastry and fold the edge of the pastry case over the top and seal.

9. Glaze the top with egg and prick through the pastry to allow steam to escape.

10. Bake in oven at Gas Mark 4/180°C/350°F for 2½-3 hours.

11. Turn out to cool. Store in an airtight tin until required.

Other European countries followed: Scotland in 1660, Germany and Denmark about 1700, Russia in 1706, England in 1752 and Sweden in 1753.

As a Christian festival New Year has been chiefly celebrated with ringing of church bells to greet the New Year and the holding of watch-night services.

Hogmanay

One place where New Year is celebrated with great activity is Scotland. At the time

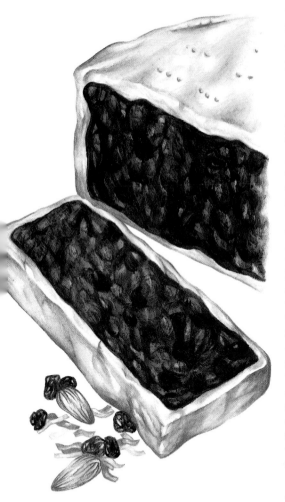

of the Reformation when any Christian festivals, other than Sunday observances, were stopped the Scots transferred their celebrations from Christmas to New Year. They call this celebration *Hogmanay*. It is not certain exactly why it is called Hogmanay but here are two possible suggestions.

In Scotland and the north of England the month of December was known as *Hagmena* from a Greek word meaning 'holy moon'. *Hagmena* — Hogmanay! The other suggestion is from the French '*homme est né — trois rois là*', meaning 'a man is born — three kings are here', referring to the visit of the wise men to Jesus. '*Homme est né*' — Hogmanay! Take your pick.

The best known ceremony attached to Hogmanay is that of *first-footing*. As the clock strikes midnight the *first-footer* knocks on the door of a neighbour's home. The rules say that the first-footer must be male, dark-haired, and not flat-footed or cross-eyed. He carries with him a lump of coal, a sprig of mistletoe, some salt, money and, in some places on the coast, a herring. He enters without speaking, puts the coal on the fire, the mistletoe on the mantelpiece, the salt and money on the table and then wishes everyone 'Happy New Year'. The visitor is then given a drink and something to eat. The gifts brought by the first-footer are symbols of heat, health, wealth and food, all of which are wished for the family in the coming year. The ceremony is a celebration of friendship and neighbourliness. No one would go to visit a neighbour at New Year or during the days that follow without taking a gift. In some parts of Scotland the party may be a *Ceilidh*, a celebration of Scottish singing and dancing. The food served at Hogmanay would usually include sandwiches, Scottish cheeses, shortbread and Black Bun.

More New Year customs

First-footing is not only practised in Scotland, but also in some other European countries where the visitor is not greeted in silence but with a great deal of noise and jollity.

Vasilopitta

NEW YEAR CAKE Cyprus

12 oz	320 g	3 sticks	butter or margarine
12 oz	320 g	1½ cups	sugar
1½ lb	640 g	6 cups	flour
8	8	8	eggs
½ can	½ can	1 cup	evaporated milk
1 tsp	1 tsp	1 tsp	vanilla essence (extract)
2 tsp	2 tsp	2 tsp	baking powder
1 tsp	1 tsp	1 tsp	mixed spice (pumpkin spice)
			grated rind and juice of half an orange
3 oz	80 g	¾ cup	ground almonds

METHOD

1 Cream the butter and the sugar together.

2 Add four eggs and half the flour, and mix well.

3 Add the remaining ingredients except the almonds.

4 Pour the mixture into a greased 9 in./28 cm round cake tin and sprinkle the top with almonds.

5 Bake in oven at Gas Mark 3/160°C/325°F for 1½ hours until a fork pushed to the bottom comes out clean.

6 When cool, mark the number of the year on the top in cream or icing (or confectioners) sugar.

In Germany New Year's Eve is a time for parties with friends and neighbours. Great buffets are served with frankfurters and potato salad, open sandwiches, pâté, and brandysnaps. In some parts of Germany everyone leaves their home at midnight and goes to the village or town square where the local band plays and fireworks are set off.

In Austria, where pigs are thought to bring good luck, miniature pigs are given at New Year as tokens of good wishes.

In Canada some people enjoy progressive suppers on New Year's Eve. These are mainly spent with close friends and family. The first course is eaten at one home and then everyone moves on to the next house for the second course, and so on, for as many stops as people can manage.

Looking back, looking forward

New Year is traditionally a time for reflecting on the past year and looking forward to the year to come. It is a good opportunity for letting go of resentments or sadnesses, for being thankful for good things past and putting into God's hands the coming year. As a family make time at New Year to share together in some way. Maybe each person could recall from the past year their most happy, frightening, sad and exciting moment. Then each could share a hope for the coming year and all pledge their help in seeing these hopes come about. Perhaps young children could make a scrapbook of the important events of the past year both at a personal and a national level.

As we look into a new year this lovely prayer is appropriate:

Teach us, Lord,
to serve you as you deserve,
to give and not to count the cost,
to fight and not to heed the wounds,
to toil and not to seek for rest,
to labour and not to ask for any reward
save that of knowing that we do your will.
IGNATIUS LOYOLA

Shortbread

Scotland

6 oz	175 g	1½ cups	plain flour
4 oz	125 g	½ cup	butter or margarine
2 oz	50 g	¼ cup	castor (table) sugar

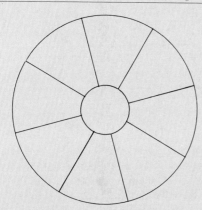

This traditional way of cutting shortbread is called Petticoat Tails.

METHOD

1 Rub the butter into the flour and sugar.

2 Knead to a smooth dough.

3 Press into a greased 7 in./18 cm round cake tin.

4 Prick surface with a fork.

5 Bake in oven at Gas Mark 3/170°C/325°F for 35-40 minutes.

6 Mark into pieces but leave in the tin for 5 minutes before turning out on to a cooling tray.

7 Store in an airtight container.

New Year Cookies

Russia

This is an old Mennonite recipe brought to Canada by Russian immigrants.

1 tsp	1 tsp	1 tsp	sugar
2 fl oz	50 ml	¼ cup	warm water
2 tsp	2 tsp	2 tsp	dried yeast
12 fl oz	325 ml	1½ cups	warm water
12 fl oz	325 ml	1½ cups	warm milk
½ tsp	½ tsp	½ tsp	salt
½ oz	15 g	1 tbsp	butter
2	2	2	eggs
8 oz	225 g	1 cup	raisins
			sufficient plain flour to make a fairly thick batter

METHOD

1 Dissolve the sugar in the small quantity of water and sprinkle the yeast on top. Leave it to stand for about 10 minutes, until it goes frothy.

2 Add the other ingredients together and stir in the yeast mixture.

3 Add sufficient flour to make a fairly thick batter.

4 Allow to rise until doubled in bulk.

5 Fry spoonfuls in hot oil until golden brown. Remove and drain on absorbent paper.

6 When cool, roll in sugar and serve.

TWELFTH NIGHT

*O*n the twelfth day of
   Christmas,
my true love sent to me
twelve drummers drumming.

The prospect of twelve drummers drumming may not be a very welcome one to most households today — it would be too much for most of us to cope with. It may not have been such a daunting prospect for homes two hundred years ago, when this was a real party night. In many countries Twelfth Night marks the end of the Christmas season. Decorations come down and are packed away for another year and there is a degree of relief and sadness felt as yet another Christmas is finished.

Really Twelfth Night does not mark an ending, it tells of a beginning. In the church the day that follows Twelfth Night is called *Epiphany*, which means 'manifesting'. It recalls the showing of Jesus to the three wise men who had travelled a very long way following a star.

Wise men, they came to look for wisdom,
finding one wiser than they knew;
rich men, they met with one yet richer —
King of the kings, they knelt to you:
   Jesus our wisdom from above,
   wealth and redemption, life and love.

Guests of their God, they opened
   treasures,
incense and gold and solemn myrrh,
welcoming one too young to question
how came these gifts, and what they were,
   Gift beyond price of gold or gem,
   make among us your Bethlehem.

©CHRISTOPHER IDLE/Jubilate Hymns

Gâteau des Rois (1)

France

8 oz	225 g	2 sticks	butter or margarine
5 oz	150 g	1¼ cups	icing (confectioners) sugar
3 oz	75 g	¾ cup	plain flour
3 oz	75 g	¾ cup	ground rice (substitute with flour if unavailable)
			grated rind of 1 lemon
6	6	6	egg yolks
3	3	3	egg whites

BUTTER ICING:

3 oz	75 g	6 tbsp	butter or margarine
6 oz	150 g	1½ cups	icing (confectioners) sugar
			juice of half a lemon

METHOD

1 Cream together the butter and lemon rind.

2 Beat in the icing sugar.

3 Sift the flour and ground rice together and add one third to the mixture.

4 Add two egg yolks and mix in, then add a further third of the flour and rice mixture. Continue until all the egg yolks, flour and rice are blended.

5 Beat the egg whites until stiff and fold into the other mixture.

6 Turn into two greased 10 in./25.4cm cake tins and bake at Gas Mark 4/180°C/350°F for about one hour or until firm to the touch. Allow to cool.

7 Make up the butter icing by mixing together the three ingredients and beating until smooth. Sandwich the two cakes together and spread a layer of icing on top. Decorate as desired with three crowns, a king or a star.

These travellers are often called kings. No one knows for sure but they were certainly rich because they brought expensive gifts of gold, frankincense and myrrh.

Many years ago, before the calendar we use today came into being, 6 January was celebrated as Christmas Day. In countries where Christians belong to the Orthodox church this is still the case. And in Ireland Epiphany is known as Little Christmas and is still a holiday for most people.

In Russia a lady known as 'Baboushka' (or 'granny') brings gifts for children on 6 January. The story tells how Baboushka was visited by the three kings searching for Jesus. She welcomed them into her home and fed them, but when they asked her to go with them to find him she declined, saying she was too busy. Eventually she did set off with toys for the new baby but she was too late, he had moved on. It is said that Baboushka is still searching and whenever she finds a home with a child she leaves a toy — just in case!

Gâteau des Rois (2)

France

8 oz	225 g		*puff pastry*
4 oz	100 g		*marzipan (or almond paste)*
2 oz	50 g	½ cup	*icing (confectioners) sugar*
			juice of 1 lemon
			few nuts and cherries

METHOD

1 Divide the pastry in two and roll out both pieces into rounds.

2 Roll out the marzipan into a round of the same size.

3 Put marzipan on one of the rounds of pastry, sprinkle over the nuts and cherries. Place the other pastry round on top and seal the edges.

4 Allow to rest for 30 minutes then bake at Gas Mark 8/230°C/450°F for 25 minutes, until well risen and golden brown in colour.

5 Allow to cool then ice with icing made from the icing sugar and enough lemon juice to mix to a spreading consistency.

6 Decorate as cake no. 1.

In Italy there is a similar story, this time with a character called Befana. Her name is thought to be a corruption of the word Epiphany. Befana is the bringer of gifts to Italian boys and girls.

In Norway and Poland boys dress up as wise men and, carrying stars held high on poles, go from house to house singing carols and collecting money or sweets in return.

The tradition of a Twelfth Night cake goes back seven hundred years. In England it is mentioned in the royal accounts at the court of Edward II. In France in the thirteenth century the monks of Mont St Michel are known to have celebrated with a cake known as *Gâteau des Rois*. There are various customs attached to this cake and many recipes for it. However, the main purpose is to choose a king and queen to rule over the party celebrations. This is done by putting a dry bean into the cake. Whoever gets the piece with the bean becomes the king. He then chooses himself a queen. If a lady receives the bean she chooses herself a king. Sometimes a child sits under the table and calls out the name of each person to be served with the next piece of cake. The king and queen are given crowns to wear, all others present choose a ticket from a dish with the name of the character they are to be — such as Sir Gregory Goose, Duchess of Daffodil, Miss Tink-a-Tink, Tom Tough and so on.

In France the Gâteau des Rois usually has three kings on top. These can still be bought in French shops. But a cut-out king or even three crowns can be used if you make your own cake. These could be gold for the gift of gold which signifies Jesus' kingship; white for the gift of frankincense which signifies Jesus' holiness; and purple for the gift of myrrh which signifies Jesus' death.

If you do follow the custom of putting away the decorations on 6 January it is a good idea to leave something special on the tree or hidden somewhere for the children to find. This not only helps with the disappointment of seeing the finery packed away but also acts as a reminder that Epiphany is about gifts: those brought by the wise men, but more especially the most wonderful gift of all — God's gift of Jesus to the whole of mankind.

MOTHERING SUNDAY AND MOTHER'S DAY

MOTHERING SUNDAY AND MOTHER'S DAY

There are two quite separate festivals kept to honour mothers: Mothering Sunday, which is kept in many places, and Mother's Day, which is celebrated in America and Canada.

Whatever we call the day and whether we celebrate it in Lent or in May the sentiment is the same. We each want to say 'Thank You' to our mother for all she means to us. This can be done first and foremost by being together and enjoying sitting down to a meal as a family. Children can give special gifts to their mothers — something home-made can often mean more than shop-bought presents. Home-made cards, perhaps made with flowers pressed the previous summer, will be much loved. Even better, what about Dad and the children cooking the dinner that day? There are a couple of simple menu suggestions on the next page.

A special grace
Begin the meal with one of the children saying grace, maybe something like this:

Loving Father,
Today we want to thank you
for the love we receive every day from
* Mummy/Mum/Mother,*
for the love we share as a family,
and for the food we are about to eat.
Through Jesus our Lord.   Amen.

Children can have fun writing out and decorating the menu card. This can be displayed on the dining table next to a small vase of flowers.

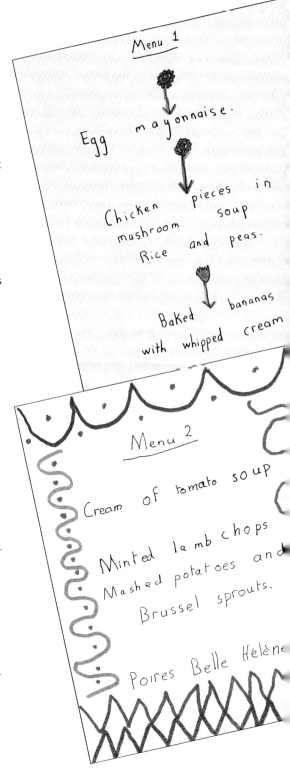

Menu 1
Egg mayonnaise.
Chicken pieces in mushroom soup
Rice and peas.
Baked bananas with whipped cream

Menu 2
Cream of tomato soup
Minted lamb chops
Mashed potatoes and Brussel sprouts.
Poires Belle Hélène

Egg mayonnaise

1 Take one hard boiled egg per person and cut in half.
2 Shred a little lettuce on a small plate and place the two halves of the egg on top.
3 Spoon over enough mayonnaise to coat the eggs.
4 A little paprika sprinkled on top looks good.

Chicken pieces in mushroom soup

1 Put the chicken pieces in a large casserole and cover with the soup.
2 Cook in the oven at Gas Mark 4/180°C/350°F for one hour until the chicken is tender. Large pieces may take a little longer.

Baked bananas

1 Take one large banana per person.
2 Cut in half lengthways and lay them side by side in a heatproof dish.
3 Sprinkle with demerara (or turbinado) sugar to cover the bananas.
4 Bake at Gas Mark 4/180°/350°F for ten minutes. You can put these in as you sit down to your main course, but don't forget them.
5 Serve hot with whipped cream.

The children should be able to help with this, particularly with the first course and the dessert.

Tomato soup

1 Heat as instructed on the packet or can.
2 As you serve it put in a spoonful of cream or yoghurt. It gives the professional touch!
3 Serve with bread or rolls.

Minted lamb chops

(You need to get these ready early in the day to allow at least 2-3 hours marinading.)
1 Take one chop per person — two if they are small loin chops — and place in a flat-bottomed dish.
2 Mix together: 2 tbsp olive/cooking oil
        Juice and rind of one lemon
        Crushed clove of garlic (optional)
        1 tsp chopped mint
        salt and pepper.
3 Spoon the mixture over the chops, turning them from time to time, over a period of 2-3 hours. Grill (broil) the chops on both sides for about 20 minutes, until they are tender and cooked through, then serve with the vegetables.

Poires Belle Hélène

1 Put the contents of a tin of pears, minus the juice, into individual serving dishes and set on one side.
2 Make the chocolate sauce:
        2 oz/50 g/2 squares chocolate (semi-sweet baking chocolate)
        4 tbsp golden (or corn) syrup
        ½ oz/15 g/½ tbsp butter or margarine
   Heat all ingredients together gently, stirring continuously.
3 Serve the pears with a scoop of ice cream and pour the hot sauce over the top.

Shrewsbury Simnel Cake

England

CAKE:

6 oz	175 g	1¼ sticks	butter or margarine
6 oz	175 g	¾ cup	sugar
8 oz	225 g	2 cups	plain flour
1½ tsp	1½ tsp	1½ tsp	baking powder
3	3	3	eggs
1 lb	450 g	3 cups	mixed dried fruit
2 oz	50 g	½ cup	chopped almonds
2 oz	50 g	½ cup	cherries
2 oz	50 g	½ cup	mixed peel
2 tbsp	2 tbsp	2 tbsp	milk
1 tsp	1 tsp	1 tsp	mixed spice (pumpkin spice)

ALMOND PASTE:

8 oz	225 g	2 cups	ground almonds
4 oz	100 g	1 cup	icing (confectioners) sugar
4 oz	100 g	½ cup	castor (table) sugar
1 tsp	1 tsp	1 tsp	lemon juice
2 drops	2 drops	2 drops	almond essence (extract)
1	1	1	beaten egg

METHOD

1 Cream the butter and sugar together.

2 Sieve the flour, baking powder and mixed spice together.

3 Beat the eggs and add, one at a time, with a spoonful of the flour, into the butter and sugar mixture.

4 Add all the other ingredients and fold in carefully.

5 Make the almond paste.
Mix almonds, icing sugar and castor sugar together. Add lemon juice, almond essence and enough egg to form a fairly dry paste.

6 Cut the almond paste in two and roll out one half to the size of the 8 in./20 cm diameter cake tin.

7 Put half the cake mixture into the greased tin, then place the almond paste layer on top of that before adding the rest of the cake mixture.

8 Bake in oven at Gas Mark 2/150°C/300°F for 2-2½ hours. This is difficult to test with a fork to see if the cake is cooked as the almond paste is sticky when hot. Press the cake with a finger, it should be firm.

9 Allow to cool in the tin for a short while before turning out.

10 When cool, decorate with the remaining almond paste. A traditional way is to put 11 balls around the top edge, to represent the Apostles minus Judas, who betrayed Jesus.

Bury Simnel Cake

England

5 oz	150 g	1¼ cups	plain flour
½ tsp	½ tsp	½ tsp	baking powder
1 oz	25 g	2 tbsp	butter
1 oz	25 g	2 tbsp	lard
3 oz	75 g	⅓ cup	castor (table) sugar
½ tsp	½ tsp	½ tsp	ground cinnamon
1 tsp	1 tsp	1 tsp	ground nutmeg
8 oz	250 g	1½ cups	currants (or raisins)
1 oz	25 g	2 tbsp	chopped candied peel
1	1	1	beaten egg
2-3 tbsp	2-3 tbsp	2-3 tbsp	milk
			whole blanched almonds
			cherries

METHOD

1 Rub the butter and lard into the flour and add the sugar, spices, chopped peel and currants.

2 Add the egg and mix into a very stiff dough, adding some of the milk if necessary.

3 Form the dough into a round flat cake and put it on to a greased baking tray. Decorate with the nuts and cherries.

4 Bake in oven at Gas Mark 6/200°C/400°F for 30 minutes or until golden brown.

5 Cool on a cooling tray and serve.

Mothering Sunday

Mothering Sunday always falls on the fourth Sunday in Lent and can bring a welcome bit of brightness in churches where the custom is to have no flowers during Lent. Many churches present baskets of posies collected by the children during the previous day to all the mothers. There are differing views about the origin of Mothering Sunday. Some say that the custom originated in honouring the 'Mother Church' and parishioners travelled to the main church or the cathedral to worship on this day. The other view is that it was a holiday to allow young girls and boys in service at big houses and farms to visit their mothers. This came six months after the main hiring fairs in October. Often the girls were allowed by their employer to make a special cake to take home. This was called Simnel cake and would sometimes be kept by the mother for the Easter celebrations. Walking home, the young people picked flowers from the hedgerows and fields to make posies for their mothers.

Coming in the middle of Lent, Mothering Sunday was an opportunity to relax the rigours of fasting and richer food would be served. Two traditional delicacies were Lamb's Tail Biscuits and Fig Pie (see page 42).

The Simnel cake

The origin of the Simnel cake is recorded in a Shropshire legend. The story is told of Simon and Nell who both wanted to make a cake to give to their mother. Unfortunately they could not agree how to cook the cake. Simon wanted to boil it and Nell wanted to bake it. In the end they decided to do both and produced a rather solid indigestible cake. They probably argued about the name as well and settled on Sim-Nel, and so we have the Simnel cake!

There are several different kinds of Simnel cake. The Devizes Simnel is made in the shape of a star but the Bury Simnel is a flat spiced cake. The best known of all is the Shrewsbury Simnel with a central layer of marzipan in a rich fruit cake.

Lamb's Tail Biscuits

England

6 oz	175 g	1½ cups	plain flour
3 oz	75 g	6 tbsp	butter or margarine
½ tsp	½ tsp	½ tsp	baking powder
½ tsp	½ tsp	½ tsp	salt
3½ oz	90 g	⅓ cup	castor (table) sugar
1	1	1	egg
1 tsp	1 tsp	1 tsp	cinnamon

METHOD

1 Mix the flour, baking powder and salt, and rub in the butter.

2 Add the sugar and the cinnamon.

3 Mix to a soft dough with the beaten egg.

4 Roll out on a floured surface to ¼ in./0.6 cm and cut into lamb's tail shapes.

5 Place on a greased baking tray and bake in oven at Gas Mark 3/160°C/325°F until golden brown.

6 Cool on a cooling tray and dust with icing (confectioners) sugar.

Fig Pie

England

One 8 in. pastry case (ready-made pie crust) baked blind. For pastry recipe see Black Bun (page 30).

FILLING:

1 lb	450 g	2 cups	figs cooked and chopped
2 oz	50 g	¼ cup	currants (or raisins)
6 oz	175 g	¾ cup	sugar
½ tsp	½ tsp	½ tsp	mixed spice (pumpkin spice)
1 tbsp	1 tbsp	1 tbsp	grated orange rind
1 tbsp	1 tbsp	1 tbsp	black treacle (dark molasses)
2	2	2	egg whites

METHOD

1 Whisk the egg whites until stiff.

2 Mix all the other ingredients, then fold in the egg whites gently.

3 Pour into baked pastry case and bake in oven Gas Mark 5/190°C/375°F for 20 minutes until golden brown.

4 Serve cold with whipped cream.

Mother's Day

In 1900 Miss Anna Jarvis of America decided that mothers were doing such an important job they should be honoured by their own special day. On this day they should be given flowers and waited upon. The idea grew and before long the Congress of the USA officially decided on the second Sunday in May as Mother's Day. In America and Canada many people honour their mothers by wearing carnations, a red one if their mother is still alive, a white one if she has died and a pink one in honour of step-mothers.

EASTER

Shrove Tuesday Buns

Scandinavia

These are eaten in several countries and vary slightly from place to place. In Sweden they are called *Semlors* and in Finland *Laskiais-pullia*. Here is a very simple way of making them.

FOR EACH PERSON:

			2 currant buns or soft round rolls
2 oz	50 g	1 tbsp	almond paste
			slightly sweetened whipped cream
			icing (confectioners) sugar
			cinnamon
			bowl of warm milk

METHOD

1 Cut off the tops of the buns and scoop out some of the middle.

2 Fill with almond paste.

3 Top with a good serving of whipped cream.

4 Replace the tops of the buns and dust with icing sugar.

5 Serve in soup bowls half filled with warm milk and sprinkle with cinnamon.

LENT

Shrove Tuesday heralds Lent, which begins the following day, Ash Wednesday. The name *Lent* comes from the Old English word *Lengten* which simply refers to the lengthening of days and the coming of spring. It is, however, a very specific season in the church's year, and lasts for forty days. Sundays are feast days and therefore do not count, so Lent finishes on the eve of Easter. The forty days are a reminder of the time Jesus spent in the wilderness before starting his ministry. He spent this time alone with God, seeking his closeness and direction for the future. The writers of the Gospels tell us how the devil tried to persuade Jesus to go his way by tempting him with popularity and power. Jesus resisted the temptation, choosing instead a way of suffering and death.

This period was once a time of preparation for new Christians who were to be baptized at Easter. Now it has become more a time of reflection for Christians, a sort of spiritual 'check-up' in the weeks before Easter, so that celebrating the death and resurrection of Jesus at Easter can come out of a heart right with God. It is therefore seen as a time of self-denial and fasting. Many people today still 'give up

A chef's hat to make

Why not make a chef's hat for the pancake maker in your house?

1 *Measure round the chef's head, and cut a piece of paper the same length plus 1 in. (2 cm), and 3 in. (8 cm) deep.*

2 *Cut a piece of crêpe paper twice as long as the plain piece and 12 in. (30 cm) deep.*

3 *Fold over the crêpe paper 2 in. (5 cm) along one edge.*

4 *Gather the crêpe paper to fit the paper band and stick it on with sticky tape.*

5 *Form the whole thing into a tube and stick.*

6 *Fold the crêpe paper inwards at the top.*

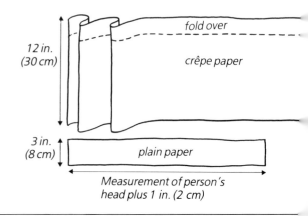

fold over

12 in. (30 cm)

crêpe paper

3 in. (8 cm)

plain paper

Measurement of person's head plus 1 in. (2 cm)

Pancakes

England

BASIC BATTER:

4 oz	100 g	1 cup	plain flour
1	1	1	egg
½ pint	275 ml	1¼ cup	milk
			oil for frying

METHOD

1 Mix the egg and half the milk with the flour until smooth.

2 Whisk in the rest of the milk.

3 Heat a little oil in a small frying pan (just enough to grease the pan, not enough for the oil to run).

4 Pour a little mixture into the pan and tip the pan to allow the mixture to cover the bottom. When the top side is drying and the underside is turning a golden brown turn the pancake over. It should really be tossed but tossing pancakes takes a bit of practice!

5 Pancakes can be kept soft and warm in a clean tea towel while the others are cooking. This mixture should make eight.

6 Traditionally they should be served rolled up with lemon juice and sugar.

Savoury Pancakes

These make a lovely change and quite a satisfying meal. Make pancakes with basic batter but fill with one of the following:

Chicken and corn: mix together diced cooked chicken and canned sweetcorn with a basic white sauce. Garnish with a little fried banana.

Minced beef and tomato: mix together some left-over minced meat with a little from a tin of tomato soup to moisten it. Fill the pancakes with this and pour the rest of the tin of soup over them. Heat through in the oven for 20 minutes at Gas Mark 5/190°C/375°F.

Bacon and cheese: chop and fry together any combination of bacon, onion, peppers and mushrooms and stuff the pancakes. Pour ½ pint/275 ml/1 cup of cheese sauce over the pancakes. Sprinkle some grated cheese on top and brown under the grill.

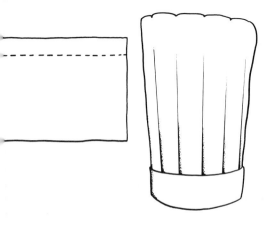

Coquille Buns

England

Coquille buns are from Norwich in England and are traditionally eaten on Shrove Tuesday.

1 lb	*500 g*	*4 cups*	*self-raising flour**
2 oz	*50 g*	*¼ cup*	*lard*
2 oz	*50 g*	*¼ cup*	*butter or margarine*
4 oz	*100 g*	*½ cup*	*sugar*
2 tsp	*2 tsp*	*2 tsp*	*mixed spice (pumpkin spice)*
2 tbsp	*2 tbsp*	*2 tbsp*	*mixed dried fruit*
1	*1*	*1*	*egg*
			a little milk

* if plain flour is used add 2 tsp baking powder

METHOD

1 Rub the lard and butter into the flour.

2 Stir in the sugar, spice and fruit.

3 Beat the egg and mix in with enough milk to make a soft dough.

4 Roll out on a floured surface to 2 in./ 5 cm thick and cut into squares.

5 Bake on greased baking trays in oven at Gas Mark 5/ 190°C/375°F for 20 minutes or until golden brown.

6 Serve split and buttered, either warm or cold.

something for Lent', others do some special reading or an extra piece of Christian service. In some Orthodox countries today, as in days gone by, the Lenten fast is a very serious thing. During the fast, no meat, cream, butter or eggs were eaten and that is why people ate pancakes on Shrove Tuesday, as a way of using up the eggs and cream which would not keep until Easter. In the north of England it is still called Collop Day (a collop being a piece of meat). At one time any meat in the house was cut up into small pieces to be dried or salted for keeping until after Easter.

So, with the coming austerity of Lent, Shrove Tuesday has traditionally become the day for a last fling. 'Carnival' literally means 'goodbye meat' and *Mardi Gras* means 'Fat Tuesday'. In Germany, as in some other European countries, both Monday and Tuesday are carnival days. In South America and the USA *Mardi Gras* is a time of great merriment. The *Mardi Gras* carnival in New Orleans is world-famous.

Greek Lenten calendar

In Greece people make a special Lenten calendar called a *Kukaras*. It is made from a potato and six feathers like this:

You pull one feather out for each week of Lent.

EASTER

After the Sabbath, as Sunday morning was dawning, Mary Magdalene and the other Mary went to look at the tomb. Suddenly there was a violent earthquake; an angel of the Lord came down from heaven, rolled the stone away, and sat on it. His appearance was like lightning, and his clothes were as white as snow. The guards were so afraid that they trembled and became like dead men.

The angel spoke to the women. 'You must not be afraid,' he said. 'I know you are looking for Jesus, who was crucified. He is not here; he has been raised from death, and now he is going to Galilee ahead of you; there you will see him! Remember what I have told you.'

So they left the tomb in a hurry, afraid and yet filled with joy, and ran to tell his disciples.

Suddenly Jesus met them and said, 'Peace be with you.' They came up to him, took hold of his feet, and worshipped him.

MATTHEW 28:1-9 Good News Bible

Easter is the most important and the most joyous of all festivals. Through the death of Jesus on Good Friday we have forgiveness of sins; in his resurrection on Easter Sunday we have a new life for ever.

Easter cards to make

Making your own Easter cards is fun and gives pleasure to those who receive them. Here are two suggestions.

1 Cut an oval in the front of the card, leaving part of the left side attached (as shown in the picture) so that the flap can be opened and closed.

2 Cut a piece of card to the shape shown in picture (a). Make a small chick out of a yellow cotton wool ball. Glue the chick to the centre of the card. Fold in both ends of the card as shown in picture (b).

Palm Sunday

Let's begin at the beginning of Holy Week (the week before Easter). On Palm Sunday we remember Jesus riding into Jerusalem on a donkey. The people who were in Jerusalem for the Passover Festival were so excited to see Jesus coming that they cut down palm branches to wave and they threw them down before him, forming a carpet for him to ride on.

This little song catches the excitement of the occasion:

Praise King Jesus, riding into town,
Riding on a donkey,
Throw your jackets down,
Sing Hosanna,
We will praise him,
Praise King Jesus riding into town

D. PARSONS © 1970 Scripture Union

In those days a king rode into battle on a horse but a king who came in peace to greet his people rode a donkey. By riding into Jerusalem, the centre of Jewish worship, Jesus was proclaiming that he was King of the Jews, and many recognized him as the Messiah, the long-awaited liberator and king. The crowds shouted 'Hosanna to the Son of David' and 'Blessed is he who comes in the name of the Lord'. The religious leaders got angry and told Jesus to stop the people shouting. 'If they do not shout,' Jesus said, 'even the stones will cry out.'

There are many traditions associated with Palm Sunday. In some places processions are held and in many churches crosses made of palm are given to the congregation. These are kept until the following year, when on Ash Wednesday some are burnt and the ashes used for marking the foreheads of the congregation, as a sign of mortality and the need for forgiveness.

Figs are traditionally eaten on Palm Sunday; and we can remind ourselves of the occasion by decorating our homes with twigs. Pussy willow is a good

Easter eggs

The custom of giving eggs is one that can be traced back as far as 900 BC to ancient China where eggs were decorated and used to signify the return of spring and the continuance of life. To the Christian the Easter egg can be a symbol of the resurrection of Jesus, and our rising with him to new life.

Coloured hard boiled eggs

1 Wrap eggs in onion skins, beetroot skins or spinach leaves. Tie into place with string, or wool (yarn).

2 Boil the eggs for 30–40 minutes and allow to cool.

3 Unwrap the eggs. If you like at this stage you can scratch patterns into the colour with a pin.

4 With a little kitchen oil on a soft cloth rub the eggs until shiny.

The eggs can be drawn on with candle wax before wrapping in skins and the pattern made by the wax will resist the dye and produce an attractive effect.

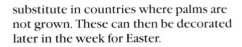

Blown eggs

Egg blowing is rather tricky to do. However, if you have the patience it is well rewarded: there is nothing inside to go bad and so the eggs can be kept for a long time. Also the lightness of the shell enables you to use blown eggs as hanging decorations.

1 Make a hole in both ends of the egg with a needle. Then with a sharp pointed knife make one hole about ¼ in. (6 mm) across.

2 With a needle make sure that the yolk inside is broken.

3 Over a bowl blow the contents of the egg out through the large hole. The eggs need not be wasted, they can be used for cooking.

4 Wash inside and out with detergent and dry.

5 The eggs can then be decorated with paint or ink. OR mix paint with liquid soap, cover the eggs and allow to dry. Then scratch patterns with a needle or skewer.

6 A coat of varnish will make them look even better, and will add a little to their strength.

Painting hard boiled eggs

Eggs can be painted with acrylic paint in patterns or faces. Gold and silver paint make very exotic eggs.

substitute in countries where palms are not grown. These can then be decorated later in the week for Easter.

Maundy Thursday

On this day Christians remember that Jesus ate the Last Supper with his disciples, sharing bread and wine with them, washing their feet and commanding them to, 'Love one another, as I have loved you'. The name Maundy comes from the Latin world *Mandatum*, meaning command. Many Christians around the world remember Jesus' Last Supper with his friends as they celebrate Holy Communion, Eucharist, the Lord's Supper, Mass or Breaking of Bread. Although it has different names it reminds all Christians of the breaking of Christ's body and the pouring out of his blood for us for forgiveness of sins — a sign of a new relationship between God and man.

The washing of the disciples' feet has been commemorated in different ways. The Pope still washes the feet of twelve priests in Rome each year. In England Edward II washed the feet of fifty poor men in 1326. This tradition carried on till the early eighteenth century and from that day the reigning monarch gives purses of special coins to as many people as years of his or her age.

An Easter egg tree

Decorated in the same way as blown eggs, these look very attractive hung on twigs as an Easter tree. (See Easter day.)

Hot Cross Buns

England

1 lb	450 g	4 cups	plain flour
1 tsp	1 tsp	1 tsp	castor (table) sugar
1 tbsp	1 tbsp	1 tbsp	dried yeast
1/4 pint	150 ml	1/2 cup	lukewarm water
2 fl oz	50 g	1/4 cup	warm milk
1 tsp	1 tsp	1 tsp	salt
1 tsp	1 tsp	1 tsp	mixed spice (pumpkin spice)
2 oz	50 g	1/4 cup	castor (table) sugar
2 oz	50 g	1/4 cup	melted butter
1	1	1	egg
1 oz	25 g	1/5 cup	currants (or raisins)
1-2 oz	40 g	1/4 cup	chopped mixed peel

METHOD

1 Sieve a quarter of the flour with one teaspoonful of sugar and the yeast. Stir in the warm milk and water. Leave in a warm place for 20-30 minutes until frothy.

2 Meanwhile sieve the remaining flour with the salt and spice and add the sugar.

3 Stir the melted butter with the egg into the risen yeast. Gradually stir this into the flour and add the currants and peel.

4 Knead the dough on a floured surface until smooth. Divide into 12 and form into buns.

5 Put the buns on to greased baking trays, well apart, and allow to rise until doubled in size.

6 Make 2 slashes in the top of each bun to form a cross.

7 Bake in oven at Gas Mark 5/190°C/375°F for 15-20 minutes.

8 While still warm, glaze with 1½ tablespoonful of sugar dissolved in two tablespoonful milk.

9 Split and spread with butter and serve warm.

If you want to prepare the dough one day and cook the buns on the morning of the next, then stop after kneading the dough but before dividing it up. Put the dough into an oiled polythene bag and store overnight in the refrigerator. Then proceed as described.

GOOD FRIDAY

When they came to the place called 'The Skull' they crucified Jesus there, and the two criminals, one on his right and the other on his left. Jesus said, 'Forgive them, Father! They don't know what they are doing.' It was about twelve o'clock when the sun stopped shining and darkness covered the whole country until three o'clock: and the curtain hanging in the Temple was torn in two. Jesus cried out in a loud voice, 'Father! In your hands I place my spirit!' He said this and died.

LUKE 23:33, 34, 44-46 Good News Bible

Over a thousand years ago the Anglo Saxons, who were Christians, called the three days before Easter Day the Still Days.

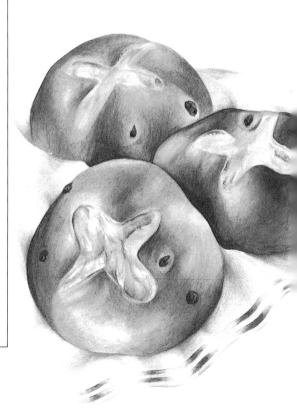

All was silent and people waited in sadness and expectancy for the joy of Easter Day. In Germany the Friday before Easter is still called *Der Stille Freitag*. Children often ask why the saddest day of the year is called Good Friday. The obvious answer is that although it is sad because we remember Jesus' death, it is also a happy day because, through his death, we can know forgiveness and be reconciled to God.

Another possible derivation is that it was originally called God's Day, reminding people that on that day God himself died on our behalf, and took away our sin, so that we can know complete and total forgiveness.

The Saxons and Danes called it Long Friday and in Danish the name is *Langfreday*. Some Eastern churches refer to the day as Great Friday, which speaks for itself.

Although Good Friday is a solemn day it is important not to let it be dull so that children grow up dreading it. For this reason it is a good idea to keep some things special to Good Friday alone. Hot cross buns (see page 50), an old English recipe, fail to be special if we eat them weeks before Easter. Some families have them for breakfast on Good Friday. If you make your own, you can get the dough all ready and let it rise slowly in the refrigerator overnight. Then bake the buns fresh for breakfast. The smell is wonderful to wake up to.

Other things which can be done on Good Friday include getting an Easter garden ready, leaving only the flowers to be added on Easter morning (see page 52). Another thing children might like to do is to make a newspaper with pictures they draw themselves, writing their own articles about the events of Easter, beginning at Palm Sunday. Alternatively, they could make a frieze on a long piece of wallpaper, telling the story in picture form. As Good Friday is still a fast day for some people, fish is often eaten as the main meal. In Cyprus they have a Good Friday soup made from Lentils and vinegar. This reminds us that as Jesus hung on the cross he was offered vinegar to drink.

Lentil Soup with Vinegar

Cyprus

1¼ lb	640 g	2¼ cups	lentils
¼	¼	¼	cabbage
1	1	1	small lettuce
2-3	2-3	2-3	spring onions
¼ pint	150 ml	½ cup	vinegar
2 tbsp	2 tbsp	2 tbsp	plain flour
2	2	2	leeks
2	2	2	cloves of garlic
			salt and pepper
			fresh coriander

METHOD

1 Wash the lentils, then boil in 1½-2 pints/900 ml/4-5 cups water.

2 Just before it comes to the boil add finely chopped cabbage, lettuce, garlic and chopped leeks.

3 Boil until all the vegetables and lentils are tender.

4 In a bowl mix the vinegar, flour, salt and pepper and stir well.

5 Add this to the soup and let it boil for two minutes.

6 Serve with croûtons of fried bread.

It is a thing most wonderful —
almost too wonderful to be —
that God's own Son should come from
* Heaven*
and die to save a child like me.

And yet I know that it is true:
he came to this poor world below,
and wept and toiled, and mourned and
* died,*
only because he loved us so.

W. W. HOW 1826-1897

Planting seeds

Planting seeds is something else you can do. A seed buried in the ground can grow into something alive and wonderful, a picture of Jesus being buried and rising to new life again.

1 Take an empty egg shell.

2 Wash it inside and out.

3 Paint a face on the outside.

4 Put some wet cotton wool (cotton balls) inside and sprinkle on some mustard and cress (or dill) seeds.

5 Water each day.

Soon it should look like this.

An Easter garden to make

1 Fill a shallow dish or tray with soil from the garden or potting compost.

2 Arrange the soil so that there is a hill on one side.

3 Cover the soil with moss, scattered cut grass or sand.

4 Make three crosses with dried twigs tied with sewing thread, and place on the hill.

5 Make a cave in the bottom of the hill for the tomb where Jesus was laid. Place a stone in front of it.

6 Make one or two little holes in the soil and put in small containers such as egg cups and then fill them with water.

7 If you like you can make a path coming from the tomb with gravel. This will remind you of the disciples running to the tomb and finding it empty on the first Easter morning.

8 On Easter day put some pretty flowers in the containers and move back the stone from the tomb, showing that it is empty.

EASTER EVE

On this day I always get the feeling that the world is holding its breath. The day before Easter Day is a day of waiting and expectation: something wonderful is going to happen, but we have got to wait. Many churches get ready by decorating with hundreds of flowers. We can prepare our homes too, with decorations and by preparation of food for the special day. For example, the twigs brought in on Palm Sunday can be decorated. They may by now be coming into leaf.

There are many different traditions in different countries as people get ready for Easter. All of them point forward with eager anticipation to the most amazing miracle the world has ever seen.

In Sweden twigs are decorated with blown eggs or painted wooden eggs, as is the custom in the USA; and in Holland they are sprayed gold or silver and hung with sweets and nuts. In Germany birch tree branches or a garden shrub are decorated with eggs; and in Switzerland branches of flowering fruit trees are brought in and decorated with ribbons and painted blown eggs. The children dance around the tree, make secret wishes, and are then invited by the adults to join them for cakes and coffee. In France, too, branches are decorated with eggs, flowers and ribbons.

In Poland, housewives prepare the food for breakfast on Easter Day, which will literally 'break the fast' of Lent. All the food is put into a basket and taken to church for a special prayer of blessing by the priest. Amongst the food will be at least one decorated hard-boiled egg. This is the first thing to be eaten on Easter Day. The head of the family takes the egg, cuts it up and passes it to all the members of the family. As they take a piece and pass it on they greet one another with an Easter greeting and some sign of the love they share as a family.

A table centre-piece to make

To make this you will need:

A ball of oasis (floral foam) about the size of a tennis ball (soaked in water)

A piece of garden cane about 12 in. (30 cm) long

A flower pot full of earth

Florist's ribbon which will tear into strips

Flowers, blossoms from cherry or apple trees, or small narcissi with stems about 1 in. (3 cm) long. Any small flowers will do

Tiny pieces of greenery

Method

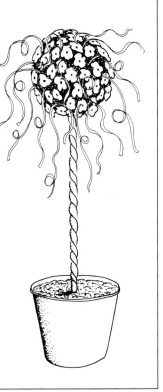

1 Cover the cane with a strip of ribbon ½ in. (1½ cm) wide. Secure one end of the ribbon with a little sticky tape, and twist it round the cane, securing the other end as before.

2 Push the ball of wet oasis onto one end of the cane and push the other end of the cane into the earth, making sure it is firm.

3 Cover the oasis with blooms, pushing the stems right into the ball.

4 Add some curls of ribbon (see Advent wreath) and some pieces of greenery.

The centre-piece can be made with artificial flowers, in which case dry oasis should be used.

German Paschal Lamb Cake

It is possible in Germany to get a special baking tin to make this delightful lamb cake which takes centre place on the table at Easter.

EASTER DAY

This joyful Eastertide
away with sin and sadness!
our Lord, the crucified,
has filled our hearts with gladness:
Had Christ who once was slain,
not burst his three day prison
our faith would be in vain —
but now has Christ arisen,
arisen, arisen, arisen.

after G. R. WOODWOOD 1848-1934 © in this version Jubilate Hymns

The day we have been waiting for has dawned. Jesus has burst out of the tomb and is alive for ever. The events of nearly two thousand years ago are brought alive once more. Easter Day can be the most exciting and inspiring day in the year. What are the ways in which we can help our children share in the joy of Easter Day?

Before doing anything else, gather the family in the living-room with the curtains still drawn and the lights off. The night before prepare a table by the window with one large candle and a small candle for each member of the family. On Easter morning all stand by the window and say the words: 'Christ has died for our sins.' Then the curtains should be thrown back and all reply: 'Alleluia! Christ is risen.'

The large candle should be lit first and then the youngest member of the family should light his or her candle from this one and pass on the light to the next youngest, and so on, until all the candles are alight. As the light is passed from one to another say, 'The light of Christ' or just 'Happy Easter.'

Paasbrod

EASTER BREAD Holland

2 tsp	2 tsp	2 tsp	dried yeast
1/2 tsp	1/2 tsp	1/2 tsp	sugar
1/2 pint	275 ml	1 cup	milk
1 tsp	1 tsp	1 tsp	mixed spice (pumpkin spice)
6 oz	175 g	1 cup	currants (or raisins) and sultanas (golden raisins)
1 oz	25 g	1 tbsp	chopped candied peel
1 oz	25 g	1 tbsp	melted butter
12 oz	325 g	3 cups	flour

ALMOND PASTE:

3 oz	75 g	1/3 cup	ground almonds
3 oz	75 g	1/3 cup	castor (table) sugar
1	1	1	egg yolk
1 tsp	1 tsp	1 tsp	lemon juice

METHOD

1 Warm the milk to blood heat (body temperature) and add the yeast and the sugar.

2 Sieve the flour and the spice into a bowl and add the yeast mixture. Mix together to form a dough, cover and leave to rise for 30 minutes.

3 Gradually work in the fruit and the melted butter.

4 Knead on a floured surface and roll out to an oblong 10 × 5 in./25 × 13 cm.

5 Mix the almond paste ingredients to form a firm paste. Roll this into a long sausage-shape and place on the rolled out dough.

6 Roll the dough round the almond paste forming the join at the bottom. Glaze with milk and put on a greased baking tray. Allow to rise until doubled in size.

7 Bake in oven at Gas Mark 6/200°C/400°F for 10 minutes, then Gas Mark 3/160°C/325°F for a further 45 minutes or until evenly golden brown.

8 Allow to cool and serve sliced with plenty of butter.

Koolitch

EASTER BREAD Russia

1 lb	450 g	4 cups	plain flour
1 tbsp	1 tbsp	1 tbsp	dried yeast
½ pint	275 ml	1 cup	milk
4 oz	125 g	½ cup	sugar
3	3	3	eggs
4 oz	125 g	1 stick	butter
4 oz	125 g	½ cup	raisins
4 oz	125 g	½ cup	dried fruit
½ tsp	½ tsp	½ tsp	salt
1 tsp	1 tsp	1 tsp	ground cardamom
½ tsp	½ tsp	½ tsp	ground cinnamon
½ tsp	½ tsp	½ tsp	ground saffron
¼ tsp	¼ tsp	¼ tsp	ground nutmeg
			icing and glacé cherries

METHOD

1 Warm the milk to blood heat (body temperature). Sprinkle on the yeast and one teaspoonful of sugar. Add half of the flour, mix well and allow to go frothy.

2 Cream the butter and sugar, then beat in the eggs one at a time. Add the yeast mixture and all the other ingredients.

3 Knead well until the dough is smooth and elastic. Cover and allow to rise until doubled in size.

4 Traditionally this bread is baked in tall cans (you can use well greased old soup, bean or coffee cans), or mould the dough to form the letters of the word 'PAX' meaning peace.

5 Bake in oven at Gas Mark 5/190°C/375°F for 20-30 minutes or until golden brown.

6 Cool on cooling tray and then decorate with icing and glacé cherries.

Easter Lamb

Greece

5 lb	2.5 kg	5 lb	leg of lamb
2	2	2	cloves of garlic
2	2	2	sprigs of rosemary
2 oz	50 g	4 tbsp	butter
8 oz	225 g	2 cups	broad (or butter) beans
4	4	4	small onions
6	6	6	medium potatoes
1 pint	575 ml	2½ cups	chicken stock
			salt and pepper

METHOD

1 Make cuts in the joint and insert the garlic.

2 Rub the meat with salt and pepper and lay the sprigs of rosemary on top.

3 Put the meat on a rack in a roasting tin, cover with the butter and roast in the oven at Gas Mark 8/230°C/450°F for 10 minutes.

4 Baste the lamb with the fat in the tin and arrange the beans, the onions and the sliced potatoes around. Pour the stock over and return to the oven reduced to Gas Mark 4/180°C/350°F for 2-2¼ hours until tender. Serve hot.

Salatá de Cartofi

POTATO AND OLIVE SALAD Romania

I have included this salad as it goes particularly well with lamb, which is a traditional dish in many places at Easter. It could be served with the Greek *Easter Lamb* dish, leaving out the sliced potatoes.

1 lb	½ kg	1 lb	cold boiled potatoes
1 bunch	1 bunch	1 bunch	spring onions
2 oz	50 g	¼ cup	black olives
2 oz	50 g	¼ cup	green olives
3	3	3	hard boiled eggs
1	1	1	small washed lettuce, shredded

DRESSING:

2 tbsp	2 tbsp	2 tbsp	water
1 tsp	1 tsp	1 tsp	castor (table) sugar
3 tsp	3 tsp	3 tsp	vinegar
			olive oil

METHOD

1 Slice the potatoes. Chop the onions and cut the eggs into wedges. Mix together with the olives and lettuce.

2 Mix the water, sugar and vinegar together and toss the salad in it.

3 Sprinkle liberally with olive oil.

When everybody has a lighted candle say together: 'He is risen indeed. Alleluia!'

The candles can then be blown out and breakfast — (boiled eggs!) — can begin. Do not forget to put flowers on the Easter garden (see page 52) and to remove the stone from the front of the tomb.

Having prepared for forty days for the coming of Easter, it is indeed a day to celebrate. One fairly universal tradition is the giving of Easter eggs. Let's look at how different people give their eggs.

In Germany the children put out nests of moss in the garden hoping to find eggs in them (and, of course, the parents oblige!), whereas in Italy painted eggs are hidden in the garden, some with long strings attached to them to help the children find them.

In Greece red-coloured eggs are carried on Easter Day and when two people meet they bang their eggs together and say 'Christ is risen.'

In France decorated eggs are brought by the Easter Bells and hidden under baskets and in trees.

In North Carolina in the USA Easter egg fights are held. Coloured hard-boiled eggs are banged together to see which breaks first.

In Georgia in the USA twenty-thousand decorated hard-boiled eggs are hidden in the woods near Stone Mountain. Hundreds of children between the ages of three and nine hunt for them.

In South Africa eggs are hidden in the garden and sometimes a treasure hunt is worked out, giving clues to help people find them. The winner of the treasure hunt is given a big egg as a prize.

In Poland *pysanki* eggs are made. *Pysanki* means to scratch and refers to the patterns scratched into beeswax which is used to cover the hard-boiled eggs. When the eggs are dyed the pattern remains. The first egg is always decorated with a ploughsharc design to signify the beginning of farm work in the spring.

Egg rolling is another ancient custom found in different countries. In England it is done in Preston and in America on the lawn of the White House. Some say this custom is to remind us of the rolling away of the stone from the tomb of Jesus.

Chocolate Easter eggs first became popular about 150 years ago and are now quite universally enjoyed. A word of caution about hiding these in the garden — they do melt if they are not in the shade.

In some countries, of course, Easter does not coincide with spring but with autumn. In Australia and New Zealand this is the case and they celebrate Easter at the same time as harvest and reaping. In Sydney there is a big agricultural show called the Royal Easter Show where they display flowers, fruit, vegetables, livestock, and arts and crafts. The evening is finished off with a grand firework display.

Easter Biscuits

England

8 oz	225 g	2 cups	plain flour
pinch	pinch	pinch	salt
½ tsp	½ tsp	½ tsp	mixed spice (pumpkin spice)
3 oz	75 g	6 tbsp	butter or margarine
3 oz	75 g	¼ cup	castor (table) sugar
1	1	1	egg, beaten
3 oz	75 g	½ cup	currants (or raisins)

METHOD

1 Sieve the flour, salt and spice together.

2 Cream the butter and sugar until light and fluffy.

3 Beat in a little egg and flour.

4 Stir in the currants and the remaining flour to make a stiff dough.

5 Roll out on a floured surface to ¼ in./0.6 cm thick. Cut into shapes.

6 Prick with a fork, brush with a little milk and sprinkle with castor sugar.

7 Place on a greased baking tray and bake in the oven at Gas Mark 3/170°C/325°F for 20 minutes.

8 Cool on cooling tray and store in an airtight container.

Cassata alla Siciliana

EASTER CHOCOLATE CAKE Italy

*1 Madeira cake (plain yellow pound cake),
9 × 3 in./23 × 8 cm*

1 lb	500 g	2 cups	cottage cheese
2 tbsp	2 tbsp	2 tbsp	double (or whipping) cream
2 oz	50 g	¼ cup	sugar
2½ tbsp	2½ tbsp	2½ tbsp	orange juice
2 tbsp	2 tbsp	2 tbsp	chopped candied fruit
1 tbsp	1 tbsp	1 tbsp	chopped pistachio nuts
2 oz	50 g	2 squares	chocolate (semi-sweet baking chocolate)

ICING:

12 oz	375 g	12 squares	chocolate (semi-sweet baking chocolate)
6 fl oz	175 ml	¾ cup	black coffee
8 oz	250 g	2 sticks	unsalted butter

METHOD

1 Cut the cake in ½ in./1 cm slices lengthways.

2 Beat the cheese until smooth, either by hand or using a food processor.

3 Beat in the cream, sugar and juice.

4 Fold in the fruit, nuts and grated chocolate.

5 Layer the cake and the cheese mixture with cake on top and bottom. Wrap in foil, gently pressing the layers together, and chill for 3 hours.

6 Make the icing by melting the chocolate with the coffee and beating in the butter a small piece at a time until smooth. Allow to cool until it is thick enough to spread.

7 Cover the top and sides of the cake and chill for at least 12 hours before serving.

People through the ages have responded to God's gift of forgiveness and new life at Easter by giving to the poor. These customs are called 'Dole Customs' and the money given 'Dole Money' — the word 'dole' for state benefit payments comes from the same Old English root. One such custom was started by Elizabeth and Mary Chulkhurst from Biddenden in Kent, England. These ladies born in AD 1100 were Siamese twins joined at the shoulder and hip. They died at the age of thirty-four, and left land to the village on the understanding that any revenue from that land should be used each year to give six hundred cakes to the poor. This custom is still kept and cakes are given out from a cottage window on the land. The cakes (which are more like biscuits) are stamped with a picture of the sisters along with their date of birth, 1100, and the age at which they died, thirty-four.

Marzipan Nests with chickens and eggs

You need left over marzipan or almond paste for this.

METHOD

1 Take a knob of marzipan about the size of a walnut, shape it into a nest and set on a plate.

2 Divide the remaining marzipan into pieces the size of small marbles.

3 Make these into egg shapes.

4 Take two egg shapes and stick them together to form a chick, shaping a tail and a beak.

5 Set the chick and the remaining eggs in the nest.

ASCENSION DAY

Jesus said to the disciples: 'It is not for you to know the times or dates the Father has set up by his own authority. But you will receive power when the Holy Spirit comes on you; and you will be my witnesses in Jerusalem, and in all Judea and Samaria, and to the ends of the earth.'

After he had said this, he was taken up before their very eyes, and a cloud hid him from their sight.

ACTS 1:7-9 New International Version

Ascension Day is celebrated forty days after Easter Day and so always falls on a Thursday. In some countries this is still celebrated as a public holiday. During the forty days from Easter to Ascension we remember Jesus in his 'resurrection body' meeting with his disciples at various places. On Ascension Day we celebrate Jesus' return to the Father in heaven to take his triumphant place as King.

Most of the customs and traditions associated with Ascension Day have their origins way back in history. For example, in AD 470, after a terrible plague and earthquakes, the Archbishop of Vienna set aside three days before Ascensiontide as days to ask for God's blessing on the crops and the land. The Latin 'to ask' is *rogare* and so these days have come to be known as Rogation days. This Archbishop also began a custom which is still kept today. He walked around the fields, stopping every now and then to pray. Others heard about this and the custom then became a way of showing the people the 'bounds' of the parish, in the days before maps. This became known as 'beating the bounds' as the leaders of the procession pointed out landmarks with sticks. (It also fulfilled another purpose in preventing

Crullers

Scandinavia

This is a simple recipe for this May Day treat using no yeast.

2	2	2	eggs
3 oz	75 g	1/3 cup	castor (table) sugar
			grated rind of one lemon
1/2 tsp	1/2 tsp	1/2 tsp	vanilla essence (extract)
2 tbsp	2 tbsp	2 tbsp	melted butter
2 tbsp	2 tbsp	2 tbsp	milk
7 oz	200 g	1¾ cups	plain flour
1/2 tsp	1/2 tsp	1/2 tsp	baking powder
			salt
			oil for deep frying
			icing (confectioners) sugar for dusting after cooking

METHOD

1 Beat the eggs until frothy, add the sugar gradually and continue beating until light and thick.

2 Add the vanilla, lemon rind, butter and milk, and mix well.

3 Sieve together the flour, baking powder and salt and add to the mixture to form a soft dough.

4 Roll out on a floured surface to 1/4 in./0.6 cm and cut into strips about 4 × 1/2 in./10 × 1.2 cm.

5 Heat the oil and fry the strips a few at a time until puffed and golden.

6 Drain on absorbent paper, dust with icing sugar and serve.

Maypole Cake

England

6 oz	175 g	1½ cups	self-raising flour*
6 oz	175 g	¾ cup	sugar
6 oz	175 g	1½ sticks	butter
3	3	3	eggs

* if plain flour is used then add 1½ tsp baking powder

METHOD

1 Cream the butter and sugar together.

2 Beat in the eggs one at a time.

3 Fold in the sifted flour.

4 Add a little milk if necessary to make a soft dropping consistency.

5 Put mixture into 2 greased sandwich tins (round cake pans), 7 in./18 cm in diameter.

6 Bake in the centre of the oven at Gas Mark 3/160°C/325°F for 20-30 minutes. Cool on a wire tray.

BUTTER ICING:

12 oz	325 g	3 cups	icing (confectioners) sugar, sieved
6 oz	175 g	1½ sticks	soft butter or margarine

a few drops each of lemon (yellow) and green colouring

METHOD

1 Beat the butter until soft and creamy.

2 Gradually beat in the sieved icing sugar. Add a few drops of milk if necessary but do not allow the mixture to become too soft.

3 Divide the butter icing, ⅔ to ⅓. Colour the ⅔ with a few drops of lemon colouring and the ⅓ with a few drops of green colouring.

DECORATING THE CAKE

1 Sandwich the cake together with half of the yellow icing and spread the rest around the sides.

2 Spread the green icing on top and rough it up with a fork to look like grass.

3 Take a knitting needle and fix 10 in./25 cm lengths of yellow, green and white ribbon to the top. Wind the ribbons around the top of the needle and then stick the point into the cake leaving about 6 in./15 cm above the cake. Arrange the ribbons attractively around the cake.

unscrupulous farmers from extending their property by moving the fences.) Pauses for prayer and reading from the Bible at points on the way gave rise to names such as Gospel Oak, where the Gospel was read under an oak tree. In Germany and Austria this custom is kept, and organizations within the church carry banners in the procession. One lady I spoke to remembers carrying a white lamb on a cushion for the whole tour which lasted for about three hours. She had very tired aching arms by the time she returned home.

Well-dressing is another custom associated with Ascensiontide, as villages give thanks to God for the gift of water. The wells are 'dressed' in elaborate floral pictures. These pictures tell a story from the Bible or perhaps the life of a saint connected with the village.

At this time of the year, it is nice to celebrate seedtime as a family. Give the children a little plot of land to grow some vegetables or flowers. If you have no garden a few seeds grown in a pot can be as effective. Children will appreciate harvest thanksgiving more fully if they have something they have grown themselves to give thanks for.

This is a good time to start collecting spring flowers and herbs to press, to make

cards or gifts with later on. You don't need a super press, two pieces of flat wood with plenty of newspaper or kitchen paper will do. Then you just need to put something heavy, like bricks or large books on top.

In the northern hemisphere where May marks the coming of spring it has always been a favourite time for festivity. At one time, every village in England had a Maypole. One was set up in Aldgate in London beside St Andrew's Church. The pole was so large and the church so overshadowed that it was renamed St Andrew Undershaft and is still called the same today. Although the poles were festooned with ribbons and flowers it was not until the nineteenth century that Maypole dancing and ribbon plaiting began.

In the Acts of the Apostles we read that Jesus took the disciples to a hill where he lifted up his hands and blessed them. As he blessed them he withdrew from them and was carried up to heaven in a cloud.

To help children 'live out' this event it might be good to take them to a nearby hill for a picnic and try to imagine what it was like for the disciples. You could have some food like meringues as a reminder of the clouds or coconut pyramids to look like the hill.

Coconut Pyramids

The children can make these.

2	2	2	egg whites
4 oz	125 g	1½ cups	coconut
4 oz	125 g	½ cup	castor (table) sugar
1½ oz	35 g	⅓ cup	plain flour

METHOD

1 Whisk the egg whites until stiff.

2 Fold in the other ingredients very carefully using a metal spoon.

3 Put 12 spoonfuls of mixture on to a greased baking tin and, using two forks, form them into mountains.

4 Bake at Gas Mark 5/190°C/375°F for 10-15 minutes.

5 Cool on a cooling tray.

Meringues

2	2	2	egg whites
4 oz	125 g	½ cup	castor (table) sugar

METHOD

1 Whisk the egg whites until stiff.

2 Add half the sugar and continue whisking until the mixture stands in stiff peaks.

3 Fold in the remaining sugar with a metal spoon.

For shells — put spoonfuls on to baking parchment on a baking tray

For nests — make a circular base about 2 in./5 cm across with a little meringue. Build up walls to make nests.

4 Meringues don't need cooking, they really just need drying out. So set oven at lowest possible temperature and place meringues in the coolest part — usually the lowest shelf — and leave for 2-3 hours.

5 When cooked allow to cool on a cooling tray.

6 Sandwich shells together with whipped cream.

7 Fill nests with whipped cream and fruit.

WHITSUN

*W*hen the day of Pentecost had come, they were all together in one place. And suddenly a sound came from heaven like the rush of a mighty wind, and it filled all the house where they were sitting. And there appeared to them tongues of fire, distributed and resting on each one of them. And they were all filled with the Holy Spirit and began to speak in other tongues, as the Spirit gave them utterance.

ACTS 2:1-4 Revised Standard Version

Pentecost is the name of the Jewish festival that was being celebrated in Jerusalem when the Holy Spirit first came to the disciples. Pentecost came fifty days after the Passover (the Greek word *penteconta* means fifty) and is also called the Feast of Weeks or *Shevuoth*. For the Jews it was originally a spring festival celebrating the first-fruits of the wheat harvest, and was introduced after their release from Egypt. It also commemorates the giving of the Law to Moses on Mt. Sinai — as a reminder of this most important event the Jews eat cakes shaped like mountains with white toppings to look like clouds.

It is said that the people waited so long for Moses to return from Mt. Sinai that the milk curdled and white cheese was left, and so dishes such as cheese *blintzes* (see page 63), and cheese *knishes* (see page 62) and cheesecakes are traditionally eaten at *Shevuoth*. The whiteness of these

Cheese Knishes

Jewish

DOUGH:

8 oz	225 g	2 cups	plain flour
1 tsp	1 tsp	1 tsp	baking powder
½ tsp	½ tsp	½ tsp	salt
2 tbsp	2 tbsp	2 tbsp	water
1 tbsp	1 tbsp	1 tbsp	vegetable oil
2	2	2	beaten eggs

FILLING:

8 oz	225 g	1 cup	cottage cheese
4 tbsp	4 tbsp	¼ cup	thick sour cream*
1 tbsp	1 tbsp	1 tbsp	bread crumbs
1 tbsp	1 tbsp	1 tbsp	melted butter
1 tbsp	1 tbsp	1 tbsp	sugar
1 tbsp	1 tbsp	1 tbsp	raisins
1	1	1	egg, well beaten

* Natural yoghurt may be used in place of the sour cream.

METHOD

1 Mix the flour, baking powder and salt.

2 Add the water, oil and eggs and form into a smooth dough.

3 Roll out the dough on a floured surface to ⅛ in./0.3 cm and cut into 4 in./10 cm circles or squares.

4 Mix the filling ingredients all together and put a spoonful of filling on each piece of dough.

5 Damp the edges of the dough with water and fold over and seal the edges, to form half circles or triangles.

6 Place carefully on a greased baking tray.

7 Bake in oven at Gas Mark 4/180°C/350°F for about 20 minutes or until browned and crisp.

8 Serve hot or cold.

dishes also serves as a reminder of the purity or holiness of God's Law. This may also account for the tradition of cheese rolling in Gloucestershire. At Cooper's Hill, near Birdlip, England, cheeses are rolled from the top of the hill and men chase them, the catcher keeping the cheese as his prize.

In England this church festival is known as Whitsun and as Whit Monday used to be a public holiday many local games and customs grew up. In Chester in the medieval period the local Guilds presented plays taken from Bible stories in a way that ordinary people could understand. These Mystery or Miracle plays have enjoyed a recent revival.

The name Whitsun might have originated from an old custom, no longer practised, of new Christians who had been baptized at Easter wearing white for church until the celebration of Pentecost. So 'White Sunday' became Whitsun. In Scandinavian countries the term Whitsun is used. In France the name is *Pentecote*; and, in Italy, *Pentecosta*.

The Holy Spirit is described in the

Cheese Blintzes

Russian Jewish

Blintzes are filled pancakes which are fried a second time after being filled. So you will need pancakes made as per Shrove Tuesday.

FILLING:

8 oz	225 g	1 cup	cottage cheese
1	1	1	egg yolk
½ tbsp	½ tbsp	½ tbsp	melted butter
			salt, sugar and cinnamon to taste

METHOD

1 Make the filling by mixing all ingredients together.

2 Place a spoonful of mixture in the centre of each pancake and fold the edges over to form an envelope.

3 Fry the blintzes in hot butter or oil on both sides.

4 Serve hot with added sugar and cinnamon if desired.

Fruit Brûlée

France

large tin			plums or any other fruit
8 oz	225 ml	2 cups	Greek strained yoghurt (or a high-fat yoghurt)
2 oz	2 tbsp	2 oz	double cream (or whipping cream), whipped
4 tbsp	4 tbsp	4 tbsp	soft brown sugar

METHOD

1 Put the fruit into a heatproof dish with a little juice to add moisture.

2 Fold the yoghurt and cream together and spread over the fruit. Chill until just before serving.

3 Sprinkle the sugar over the yoghurt and grill (broil) until the sugar melts.

4 Serve immediately.

Milk and Honey Cookies

Jewish

God described the land he promised to the Jews as one that was flowing with milk and honey.

5 tbsp	*5 tbsp*	*5 tbsp*	*peanut butter*
5 tbsp	*5 tbsp*	*5 tbsp*	*honey*
10 tbsp	*10 tbsp*	*10 tbsp*	*dried milk*

METHOD

1 Mix all the ingredients together.

2 Roll into little balls.

3 Roll in icing sugar and serve.

Windmills to make

1 *Draw diagonal lines across a square of paper.*

2 *Place a coin in the centre of the square and draw round it.*

3 *Cut along each of the four lines to the edge of the circle.*

4 *Use a needle to make a hole in the centre of the circle. Then make a hole in the corner of each 'sail' as shown.*

5 *Push a paper fastener through the hole in one sail from underneath. Fold over the next corner and push the fastener through that. Continue until all four corners are bent over (but not creased down) and threaded onto the fastener.*

6 *Finally, push the threaded paper fastener through the hole in the centre. Wrap the arms of the paper fastener around a 12 in. (30 cm) piece of cane.*

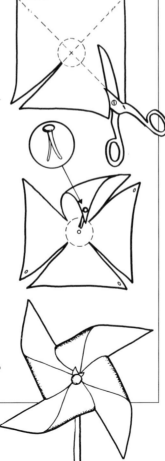

Bible as the third person of the Trinity — God the Father, God the Son and God the Holy Spirit. His presence is described in very different ways: coming as a mighty, rushing wind and tongues of fire to the Apostles at Pentecost and as a dove at Jesus' baptism, bringing peace and affirmation at the start of his ministry.

As we celebrate Pentecost or Whitsun let us remind ourselves of God's Law, which shows us where we go wrong, and the coming of the Holy Spirit who gives newness of life and power to live according to God's Law. As the Jewish people decorate their homes and food with flowers and fruit to symbolize harvest and fruitfulness after their release from bondage, so we can do the same to symbolize the harvest of God's Spirit within us and the fruit he brings forth in our lives.

The fruit of the Spirit is love, joy, peace, patience, kindness, goodness, faithfulness, gentleness and self-control.

GALATIANS 5:22, 23 Revised Standard Version

To the Holy Spirit

As the wind is thy symbol
so forward our goings.
As the dove
so launch us heavenwards.
As water
so purify our spirits.
As a cloud
so abate our temptations.
As dew
so revive our languor.
As fire
so purge our dross.

CHRISTINA ROSSETTI 1830-1894

HARVEST AND THANKSGIVING

Apple Pudding

Denmark

1½ lb	700 g	1½ lb	dessert apples
1½ oz	40 g	3 tbsp	butter
5 oz	150 g	1½ cups	fresh brown breadcrumbs
2 oz	50 g	¼ cup	soft brown sugar
¼ pint	150 ml	½ cup	natural yoghurt or cream

METHOD

1 Peel, chop and cook the apples in three tablespoonsful of water until soft — about 10 minutes. Mash roughly.

2 Melt butter in a frying pan and fry the breadcrumbs for 2-3 minutes.

3 Add the sugar to the breadcrumbs, raise the heat and cook until the crumbs are crisp. Cool on absorbent paper.

4 Stir the cream or yoghurt into the cool apple.

5 Layer the apple mixture and the breadcrumbs into individual dishes and serve.

HARVEST

*The land has yielded its harvest;
God our God has blessed us.*

PSALM 67.6 Good News Bible

Celebrating the gathering of the harvest is something which seems to have taken place around the world throughout all time. For all people the message is the same: 'no food — no life'. So harvest is a time of storing away and setting aside enough food to see the family through the winter months, whether they be dark and cold or dry and barren. It is also a time for sharing, by those who have plenty with those who have little.

God gave his people a law, recorded in the Old Testament:

When you harvest your fields, do not cut the corn to the edges of the fields, and do not go back to cut the ears of corn that were left. Do not go back through your vineyard to gather the grapes that were missed or to pick up the grapes that have fallen; leave them for the poor people and foreigners.

LEVITICUS 19.10 Good News Bible

Sharing the harvest with others can take different forms. In many churches today people bring gifts of produce which are then distributed to the elderly or the needy. In some parts of Africa Christians set aside a piece of land which they call 'God's acre'. This is cultivated through the year and the harvest is either given to those in need or sold and the money given to the poor or for the upkeep of the church.

In South India, the harvest celebration is called *Pongol*. In an area where life is often hard and food short the people are deeply grateful when the harvest is good. The first to be thanked are the animals,

A Harvest grace

All good gifts around us
are sent from heaven above:
then thank the Lord, O thank the Lord
for all his love. Amen.

(after M. CLAUDIUS 1740-1815)
JANE M. CAMPBELL 1817-1878

Harvest Loaf

1 lb	450 g	4 cups	flour (strong plain flour is best)
2 tsp	2 tsp	2 tsp	salt
½ oz	15 g	½ oz	yeast (or follow instructions on packet for dried yeast)
½ oz	15 g	1 tbsp	butter or margarine
½ pint	300 ml	1¼ cup	warm water

METHOD

1 Add salt to flour and rub in the butter.

2 Cream fresh yeast with a little of the water then add the remaining water or follow instructions on the packet of dried yeast. Stand and allow to froth.

3 Mix flour with water and yeast to a stiff dough. Knead for 10 minutes.

4 Cover and allow to rise in a warm place until doubled in bulk.

5 Shape as required. You could let the family members shape their own rolls, plaits, cottage loaves, crescents or clover leaves.
Or you could try this lovely harvest loaf. Shape two small fish and five small loaves. Set aside a small portion of dough to make a twist. Roll the remaining dough into a round flat shape about half an inch thick. For the twist, roll two long strings to fit around your main loaf shape. Brush the top with a little milk and carefully twist the two strings together and place around the edge. Position the loaves and fishes as shown.

6 Allow to rise a second time (only 10-15 minutes for the harvest loaf so that it keeps its shape).

7 Bake in the oven at Gas Mark 8/230°C/450°F for 10-15 minutes for the small rolls and 20 minutes for the harvest loaf (or until golden brown and hollow sounding when tapped).

This makes a magnificent centrepiece for a special meal.

Mobiles to make

Collecting pretty autumn leaves, fir cones, the cast-off shells of nuts, and so on, is a favourite occupation for children. But what do you do with them then? Here are two ideas:

1 Make a simple mobile with a straightened-out wire coat hanger. You will need to cut off the hook with some strong pliers and a lot of wiggling. It will look nicer if the wire is bound with strips of cloth or paper.

2 This mobile is more difficult as it needs careful balancing. It is made with either florist's stab wires or small garden sticks. The items are hung on with cotton thread tied to the stalks.

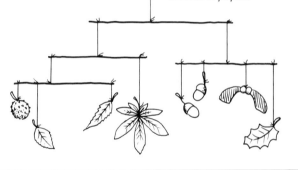

who do their part in pulling ploughs and carts. Sometimes they are thanked with a special dish of rice on the day of *Pongol*. They are also decorated with flowers and paint, the villagers dance and sing, eat special foods and thank God for his goodness.

In Fiji the harvest is of coconuts, bananas, yams and sugar cane. In Mediterranean countries it is of grapes, lemons, oranges and olives. In Australia the time of sheep-shearing is a time of celebration. In some places the main produce is oil and in others coal or fish. The celebration varies around the world. But always somewhere in the festivities are these two elements — giving thanks for the staple food of life and sharing with those in need.

Bread

Earth bore me
Water fed me
Air bathed me
Fire stirred me

I was lifted up
I was cut down
I was broken
I was burned.

Earth I was
Water bound me
Air leavened me
Fire formed me
All four elements
Of the round world
Meet in me
For man's feeding.

J.D.C. PELLOW

Apple Jelly

Harvest is a time for making the most of things that are plentiful in order to enjoy them when they are not around. With the advent of freezers some forms of preserving have almost disappeared. Jelly-making is an example. What do you do with all those apples in the autumn? Here's a suggestion.

3 lb	1.4 kg	12 cups	apples or crab apples
3 pints	1.75 l	7½ cups	water
3 lb	1.4 kg	6 cups	sugar (approx)

METHOD

1 Wash the fruit and cut up roughly. There is no need to peel or core the apples. If crab apples are used there is no need to cut up.

2 Boil the fruit and the water together for about 1 hour until the fruit is a pulp.

3 Put the pulp through a thick muslin or jelly bag overnight. I use a clean piece of old sheet tied over the legs of an upturned kitchen stool. Collect the juice in a bowl underneath.

4 Measure the juice and allow 1 lb/450 g/2 cups sugar to each pint of juice.

5 Bring back to the boil stirring until the sugar has dissolved, then boil rapidly for about ten minutes or until setting point is reached. To test put a little of the liquid onto a cold plate and cool. If it wrinkles when pushed it is ready. If not, boil a little longer.

6 Pour into clean, warm jars, cover and store.

This is very satisfying to make as it looks good and really isn't difficult. It also makes a lovely gift.

Thinking ahead

Hydrangea blooms and onion plants that have gone to seed make marvellous Christmas decorations when sprayed gold or silver. Now is the time to collect these and dry them in a warm place, to be sprayed and used later. Children might like to collect pine cones for the same purpose.

THANKSGIVING

Thanksgiving Day was first celebrated in the USA in the autumn of 1621 (apparently the celebration was three days long!). The pilgrims who had endured the dangerous Atlantic crossing from Europe to land on the east coast of North America in November 1620 were too late to plant crops to sustain them through their first winter. Many of that early colony died as a result of the hard winter and lack of food. In the spring the survivors planted seeds and they reaped their first harvest that autumn. William Bradford, the governor of Plymouth Colony, called for a day of thanksgiving and prayer. It is possible, as good Bible-reading people, that they were influenced by the Old Testament accounts of the Jewish harvest thanksgiving of *Succoth*, when the Jews were called upon by God to offer him thanks for the first harvest after their release from captivity in Egypt.

On that first Thanksgiving Day it is quite likely that turkey was eaten, as the birds lived wild and were easily captured. The women and children collected nuts and ground them with cornmeal to make bread. They also found wild plums and watercress and, together with the crops they had grown, they had a real thanksgiving feast.

The custom spread down the east coast of North America and 150 years later it had become an accepted celebration. In 1789, George Washington decreed that Thanksgiving Day should officially be kept on 26 November each year. President Abraham Lincoln proclaimed it to be an official national holiday in 1863. Since its early beginnings the date has changed several times, but by Act of Congress in 1941 Thanksgiving was fixed on the fourth Thursday in November. Canada also keeps a Thanksgiving Day, on the second Monday in October.

Today Thanksgiving is still seen as a day to thank God for all the good things of life. Some families who would not

Corn Bread

4 oz	100 g	1 cup	flour
2 tbsp	2 tbsp	2 tbsp	sugar
3 tsp	3 tsp	3 tsp	baking powder
1/2 tsp	1/2 tsp	1/2 tsp	salt
4 oz	100 g	1 cup	yellow cornmeal
1	1	1	egg
4 oz	100 g	4 oz	cooking oil or butter
10 fl oz	275 g	8 oz	milk

METHOD

1 Sieve together the flour, sugar, baking powder, salt and cornmeal.

2 In a separate bowl combine the beaten egg, oil or butter and milk.

3 Add the two together and stir until mixed, but do not over stir.

4 For 9 corn bread squares, spoon onto a greased baking tray.
For a festive ring, spoon into a greased ring mould.

5 Bake at Gas Mark 7/210°C/425°F for twenty five minutes or until golden brown.

6 Serve hot with butter.

Savoury Stuffing

Quantities for a 10-12 pound turkey are:

4 oz	100 g	4 oz	butter
4 oz	100 g	1 cup	finely chopped onion
1 lb	450 g	3 cups	finely chopped celery
3 oz	75 g	3/4 cup	finely chopped parsley
1 tsp	1 tsp	1 tsp	salt
1 tbsp	1 tbsp	1 tbsp	sage
1 tsp	1 tsp	1 tsp	paprika
1/2 tsp	1/2 tsp	1/2 tsp	pepper
1	1	1	egg
2 1/2 lb	1.8 kg	12 cups	bread crumbs

METHOD

1 Melt the butter in a frying pan.

2 Add the onion and celery. Sauté until soft.

3 Add the parsley, sage, paprika, salt and pepper.

4 Mix in the beaten egg and the bread crumbs.

5 Spoon into the neck and body cavities of the turkey. (Do not pack.)

Cranberry Sauce

1 lb	500 g	1 lb	cranberries
9 oz	225 g	1½ cups	sugar
1 pint	600 ml	2½ cups	boiling water

METHOD

1 Put all the ingredients in a pan.

2 Bring to the boil and simmer for 10 minutes.

3 Skim off the white foam.

4 Serve cold alongside the stuffing.

Pumpkin Pie

PASTRY BASE:

4 tbsp	4 tbsp	⅓ cup	corn oil
2 tbsp	2 tbsp	2 tbsp	iced water
8 oz	225 g	2 cups	plain flour
½ tsp	½ tsp	½ tsp	salt

METHOD

1 Sieve the flour and the salt into a bowl. Add the oil, and mix to a soft dough.

2 Sprinkle up to 2 tablespoons of ICED water over the mixture. If it is still too dry, add 1-2 tablespoons of cooking oil.

3 Roll out between 2 sheets of greaseproof paper to line a 9 in./23 cm pie plate.

FILLING:

2	2	2	eggs
6 oz	175 g	1½ cups	cooked, sieved pumpkin (or tinned pumpkin)
3 oz	75 g	¾ cup	sugar
½ tsp	½ tsp	½ tsp	salt
1 tsp	1 tsp	1 tsp	cinnamon
½ tsp	½ tsp	½ tsp	ginger
¼ tsp	¼ tsp	¼ tsp	ground cloves
½ pt	300 ml	1¼ cups	condensed milk or single (half and half) cream

METHOD

1 Mix all the ingredients in the above order.

2 Pour into the pastry shell.

3 Bake in a pre heated oven at Gas Mark 7/210°C/425°F for 15 minutes. Reduce temperature to Gas Mark 4/180°C/350°F and continue baking for 45 minutes.

4 Allow to cool. Serve with whipped cream or vanilla ice cream — or add the following topping to make Pecan Pumpkin Pie.

Pecan Pumpkin Pie

1½ tbsp	1½ tbsp	1½ tbsp	melted butter
3 tbsp	3 tbsp	3 tbsp	brown sugar
3 tbsp	3 tbsp	3 tbsp	chopped pecan nuts

METHOD

1 Add the ingredients together and sprinkle over the cooked pumpkin pie.

2 Brown under the grill for a few minutes.

3 Serve hot with whipped cream or ice cream.

normally say grace before a meal do so on this day in recognition of God's goodness. Some families pay special attention to saying thank you to other members of the family for their special contribution to family life. Families will try to be together for this celebration, travelling hundreds of miles to do so, and most families will invite neighbours or friends who are alone to join them for Thanksgiving dinner. However, although a guest may bring flowers for the hostess, presents are not generally exchanged.

As Thanksgiving is predominantly a recognition of an abundant harvest the dinner table is full of all the family favourite things to eat. Among these are likely to be traditional items such as roast turkey with cranberries and mashed potatoes followed by pumpkin pie with ice-cream or whipped cream. In some of the Southern states a roasted ham is eaten instead of turkey and sometimes apple pie is preferred to pumpkin. On some tables a cornucopia, horn of plenty, overflowing with fruit, flowers and vegetables makes a decorative and symbolic centrepiece. As Thanksgiving falls at the end of November it is seen by many as the beginning of the Christmas season.

God's command to the Jewish people:

Three times in the year you shall keep a feast to me.
You shall keep the feast of unleavened bread . . .
You shall keep the feast of harvest, of the first fruits of your labour, of what you sow in the field.
You shall keep the feast of ingathering at the end of the year,
when you gather in from the field the fruit of your labour.

EXODUS 23:14-16 Revised Standard Version

ALL SAINTS AND ALL SOULS

St Clement's Mousse

England

4 oz	125 g	½ cup	sugar
1 tbsp	1 tbsp	1 tbsp	powdered gelatine
4	4	4	eggs, separated
½ pint	285 ml	1 cup	whipping cream
			grated rind and juice of 2 oranges and 1 lemon

Decoration: julienne strips of orange rind blanched in boiling water for 3 minutes.

METHOD

1 Measure the two juices together and make up to ½ pint/275 ml/1 cup.

2 Put the egg yolks and sugar into a bowl over simmering water and whisk until thick and creamy — for about 10-15 minutes.

3 Put four tablespoonsful of juice into a bowl and sprinkle the gelatine on top. Leave to soak for 5 minutes. Then dissolve over a pan of hot water.

4 Stir the gelatine into the yolk mixture.

5 Add the juice and grated rind.

6 Whip the cream and egg whites separately until stiff.

7 Fold the cream into the fruit mixture then fold in the egg whites.

8 Turn into a dish and allow to set for about 4 hours.

9 Decorate.

ALL SAINTS AND ALL SOULS

On All Saints Day Christians remember the saints of the church. It is celebrated on 1 November in the West and on the first Sunday after Pentecost in the Eastern churches. The origin of the day and the accuracy of the date is difficult to establish.

The first evidence of 1 November being the date for celebrating this festival is recorded during the reign of Pope Gregory III (731-41) who dedicated a chapel in Rome on that date in honour of All Saints. In medieval England, the festival was known as All Hallows ('hallowed' means 'holy', the root word for 'saint') and the day before as Hallowe'en. Hallowe'en has since become a day connected with witches, ghosts and demons, or for trick-or-treat.

But surely it's better to celebrate goodness than evil, so how about having an All Saints party? Each guest can find out about one saint and describe that person in one minute. The Bible is a great source of information and most libraries will have books about the lives of saints. Some of the guests may be named after a saint. They could find out something about their namesake.

In the Roman Catholic and Orthodox churches the day after All Saints is celebrated as All Souls Day. On this day we can thank God for those who have gone before us, particularly members of our family. This may be a good time to get out all those old family photographs and talk, as a family, about relatives past and present. This is often the way children learn about the origins of their family.

In many countries children go from door to door singing rhymes or traditional songs in memory of the dead. The children are treated to special breads or cakes. Mexican children run through the streets with lanterns and ask for coins. This

St Gall Cheese Balls

Switzerland

4 oz	125 g	1 cup	grated mature cheddar cheese
2	2	2	eggs
½ tsp	½ tsp	½ tsp	mustard
½ tsp	½ tsp	½ tsp	paprika
2 cloves	2 cloves	2 cloves	garlic
4 oz	125 g	1 cup	plain flour
			salt and pepper

METHOD

1 Rub the cut garlic round a mixing bowl.

2 Add grated cheese, egg yolks, mustard, paprika, salt and pepper. Fork well together.

3 Whisk the egg whites until stiff.

4 Stir the egg whites and flour alternately into the cheese mixture until a softish dough is formed. Make into small balls.

5 Fry in hot fat for 5 minutes until golden, crispy and well risen.

6 Serve hot with a tomato sauce.

St Mary's Mocha Surprise

England

4 tbsp	4 tbsp	4 tbsp	drinking chocolate (chocolate drink mix)
1 tbsp	1 tbsp	1 tbsp	coffee powder (instant coffee)
4 oz	125 g	1¼ cups	fresh breadcrumbs
4 oz	125 g	½ cup	demerara (turbinado) sugar
¼ pint	150 ml	½ cup	double (or whipping) cream
¼ pint	150 ml	½ cup	single (half and half) cream
			chocolate for decorating

METHOD

1 Mix together the breadcrumbs, coffee and drinking chocolate.

2 Whip both creams together until they form soft peaks.

3 Layer the crumb mixture with the cream, finishing with a layer of cream.

4 Allow to stand for at least 8 hours.

5 Decorate with a crushed chocolate flake or chocolate curls made with chocolate (semi-sweet baking chocolate) scraped off with a potato peeler.

You could play these games, too.

Bobbing for apples

Put a number of apples in a bowl of water. Each person takes a turn at trying to catch one with their teeth, holding their hands behind them.

Snap Apple

Apples are tied on strings and hung from the door frame (with the door open!). The idea is the same as for bobbing apples—each person tries to catch an apple in their teeth without using their hands at all. This can also be done with sticky buns; it is rather messy but great fun.

Toffee Apples

England

9 or 10 firm eating apples
9 or 10 wooden skewers or sticks

1 lb	450 g	2 cups	granulated sugar
2 tbsp	2 tbsp	2 tbsp	clear honey
¼ pint	150 ml	½ cup	water

METHOD

1 Wipe the apples and remove stalks.

2 Put water, sugar and honey in a pan and stir over low heat until the sugar has dissolved.

3 Bring to the boil and boil briskly without stirring to 265°F (I find a sugar thermometer is essential for making toffee.)

4 Then reduce the heat slightly and continue boiling until the mixture reaches 310°F.

5 While the toffee is boiling push the apples on the sticks. Dip them into the toffee to coat them. Place them on a greased tin and allow to set.

tradition may be the forerunner of trick-or-treating. The Italians make special cakes called *Beans of the Dead* and in Spain they have a pastry called *Bones of the Holy*.

In Poland and Germany there is a tradition of tending and decorating graves on this day. In Poland chrysanthemums and branches from pine trees are used, and in both countries little lights or lanterns are left burning on the graves. Schoolchildren or members of the Sunday School tend those graves which are forgotten or which have no one to see to them.

As long as Thou art with Thy servants, Thy children,
they are with Thee: they lose nothing by dying.
They depart out of the world, but not out of Thy family.
They vanish from our sight, but not from Thy care.
One sun hath set upon them, but a greater is risen.
They are not dead; nay, it is death that has died in them;
 their death that is buried in their grave.
They leave behind the mortal, to put on immortality;
 theirs is entrance into healing, into rest, into glory.

From *My God, My Glory*, ERIC MILNER-WHITE.

OTHER
CELEBRATIONS

SUNDAYS

*B*y the seventh day God had finished the work he had been doing, so on the seventh day he rested from all his work. And God blessed the seventh day and made it holy, because on it he rested from all the work of creating that he had done.

GENESIS 2:2, 3 New International Version

From as early as AD 321, when the Roman Emperor Constantine made a decree against Sunday working, there have been laws regulating what should and should not be done on the first day of the week. Of course, in the Old Testament, God's command to the Jews 'to keep holy the Sabbath day' referred to the seventh day, Saturday. But, in recognition of Christ's resurrection on Sunday, Christians have adopted Sunday as their Sabbath. Many believe that God's command to the Jews about the Sabbath applies now for Christians to Sunday. In some European countries the name for Sunday is a development of the Latin *Dies Dominica* meaning Day of the Lord; so in France the name is *Dimanche*, in Italy, *Domenica* and in Spain, *Domingo*.

For Jews, celebrating the Sabbath means two things. It is a time to remember the creation of the world and a weekly reminder of the exodus from Egypt. By

Drop Scones

Scotland

8 oz	225 g	2 cups	self-raising flour*
1 oz	25 g	1 tbsp	sugar
1	1	1	egg
½ pint	280 ml	1¼ cups	milk

* if plain flour is used add 2 tsp baking powder

METHOD

1 Sieve the flour into a bowl and add the sugar.

2 Drop the egg into the flour and add a little milk. Mix with a wooden spoon until smooth.

3 Gradually beat in enough milk to produce a consistency of thick cream.

4 Heat a griddle or large frying pan and thinly butter the bottom.

5 Drop tablespoons of mixture into the pan. When bubbles rise and pop turn the scone over and cook the other side.

6 When nicely brown on both sides, allow to cool wrapped in a cloth on a cooling tray.

7 Serve with butter and jam.

stopping work on the Sabbath a Jew is testifying that God, not man, is sovereign over creation. By not picking plants or flowers, not watering the garden, not making anything, a person hands back his creative ability to God who is the creator of all things, and in a symbolic way returns all things to God's domain. Remembering the deliverance from Egypt is remembering slavery so that freedom is cherished the more.

For a Christian, making Sunday special also has two aspects: the reminder that as God rested after the work of creation, so we need to rest from our daily labour; and the celebration of Jesus' resurrection and the new life he gives. It is a time for the Christian 'family' to meet together to worship God.

Many of us can remember the very negative attitude to Sunday of our own childhood when what we did not do on Sunday seemed more important than the things we did. It's important for our children to view Sunday as a good day and not one to be dreaded. With a little thought and effort we can make it a unique day — having special things to eat, a family outing, a treat. Maybe if grace is not usually said at meal-times, to do so on Sunday would make the meal an unusual one. And taking

Scones

England

8 oz	225 g	2 cups	self-raising flour*
2 oz	50 g	¼ cup	sugar
2 oz	50 g	4 tbsp	butter or margarine
1	1	1	egg
			a little milk

* if plain flour is used add 2 tsp baking powder

METHOD

1 Rub the butter into the flour.

2 Add the sugar and stir in.

3 Beat the egg with 2-3 tablespoons of milk and mix the flour to a soft dough. Add a little more milk if necessary.

4 Roll out on a floured surface to about 1 in./2.5 cm thick and cut with 2 in./5 cm fluted cutters.

5 Place on a greased tray and bake in the oven at Gas Mark 7/210°C/425°F for about 10 minutes or until golden brown.

6 Cool on a cooling tray and serve split with butter or cream and jam.

To make **fruit scones** add 2 oz/50 g/⅓ cup of currants or raisins with the sugar.

To make **cheese scones** omit the sugar and add:

2 oz	50 g	⅓ cup	grated cheese
1 tsp	1 tsp	1 tsp	dried mustard
			salt and pepper

Chocolate Caramel Slices

New Zealand

3 oz	75 g	6 tbsp	butter or margarine
1 tbsp	1 tbsp	1 tbsp	golden (corn) syrup
4 oz	100 g	3 cups	Rice Crispies
2 × 60 g	2 × 60 g	2 × 60 g	Mars Bars (or Milky Ways)
6 oz	185 g	6 squares	chocolate (semi-sweet baking chocolate)

METHOD

1 Slowly melt the chocolate bars, butter and golden syrup.

2 Stir in the Rice Crispies and turn into a buttered tin.

3 Melt the chocolate and spread over the top.

4 Allow to set and cut into squares.

Anzacs

Australia and New Zealand

5 oz	150 g	1¼ sticks	butter or margarine
1 tbsp	1 tbsp	1 tbsp	golden (or corn) syrup
1 tsp	1 tsp	1 tsp	bicarbonate of soda (baking soda)
2 tbsp	2 tbsp	2 tbsp	boiling water
4 oz	100 g	1 cup	plain flour
4 oz	100 g	1 cup	rolled oats
4 oz	100 g	½ cup	sugar
4 oz	100 g	½ cup	raisins

METHOD

1 Melt the butter and syrup together.

2 Dissolve the soda in the boiling water and add to the mixture.

3 Mix flour, oats, sugar and raisins and pour the liquid on to them. Mix well.

4 Place teaspoonfuls on to a greased tray allowing room between for spreading.

5 Bake in oven at Gas Mark 2/150°C/300°F for about 15 minutes.

6 Leave on the tray for a few minutes before transferring to a cooling tray.

7 Store in airtight tins when cold.

care that the table looks nice and that there is time to serve the meal attractively all adds to the 'specialness'.

Activities can help too. Maybe visiting friends as a family or inviting people round, making sure that each member of the family gets a chance to suggest who the guests should be. Favourite toys, games or books kept only for Sunday can add a bit of expectation. If parents are particularly busy through the week, having time just to be a family can be vital. Even if the children are happy doing something on their own, enjoying their enjoyment is important.

Every Sabbath a Jewish father says a prayer of blessing for each of his children, beginning with the eldest. A family prayer at bedtime or after the main meal, asking God's blessing for each member of the family, can be special and uniting.

A Sunday grace

*Thank you, Father for this food,
for our family and our fun together.
Amen*

A Prayer for relaxing as a family

O heavenly Father, who blessed rest as well as labour, show us how we can relax in ways that will restore our strength and enlarge our interests, and help us always to have time to devote to playing with our family, that we may grow together and not apart as the years pass, through your love.

Amen

From *Prayers for all the Family*
GILLIAN AND ALBERT JEWELL.

BIRTHDAYS

*F**orasmuch as it hath pleased Almighty God for his goodness to give you safe deliverance, and hath preserved you in the great danger of child-birth; you shall therefore give hearty thanks unto God.*

'Thanksgiving of women after child-birth' from the *Book of Common Prayer* 1662.

This prayer from a service seldom used today suggests in its wording and tone something of the importance and drama that has always been attached to the birth of a new baby. The 'danger' the prayer speaks of is thankfully a thing of the past in most Western countries. But the enormous changes brought about by the arrival of a new life have always been the same. So there have always been customs to do with birth. Many old customs were of a superstitious nature and are fortunately not very common today; some would now be frowned on as being positively harmful to the baby! For example, in Shropshire a new baby was given butter and sugar as its first food to show riches to come. When all births took place in the home, the midwife would unlock all doors and untie any knots to ensure an easy birth. There have always been customs to try to determine what sex the child will be, and the day of the week on which a child was born has been blamed or credited with that child's personality. Today most of these superstitious customs have gone, although their influence lingers on. A silver spoon or cup used to be given as a sign of riches wished. The gift of an egg cup was seen as a wish for future fertility.

In America and Canada baby showers are popular. This is usually a surprise party given by close friends or relatives who bring gifts for the baby. If the shower is held before the baby is born the gifts are

Koeksisters

South Africa

8 oz	225 g	2 cups	plain flour
2 tsp	2 tsp	2 tsp	baking powder
1 oz	25 g	2 tbsp	butter or margarine
1	1	1	egg
4-5 tbsp	4-5 tbsp	⅓ cup	milk
			pinch salt

SYRUP:

1 lb	450 g	2 cups	sugar
½ pint	300 ml	1¼ cup	water
1 stick	1 stick	1 stick	cinnamon

METHOD

1 Rub the butter into the flour and baking powder.

2 Add the salt, egg and enough milk to form a rolling dough.

3 Roll out on a floured surface to a rectangle about 12 in./30 cm long and ¼ in./0.6 cm thick.

4 Cut into strips 3 × 1 in./7.6 × 2.5 cm. Cut each strip into three lengthways without completely cutting through at the top. Form these into plaits (braids), pinching the ends securely together.

5 Make the syrup by boiling the ingredients together, stirring until all the sugar has dissolved. Boil rapidly for one minute and set aside to cool.

6 Fry the plaits in hot oil a few at a time until they are golden brown.

7 Immediately dip them into the cold syrup and cool on a cooling tray. Serve when cool.

predominantly pale yellow, if after the birth, then it's pink for a girl and blue for a boy.

All round the world people celebrate birthdays by giving presents and having parties. Some Orthodox Christians and people in some European countries name a child after a Christian saint and so the annual celebration will then be on that particular saint's day.

In Sierra Leone in West Africa, the custom of 'outdooring' is carried out a week after the birth of a baby. On the eighth day for a girl and on the seventh day for a boy, the child is taken by an elderly member of the family to greet the world. On this occasion the child is named and then shown the sky, the clouds, trees, flowers and the street where they will later walk to school. Then the baby is introduced to the neighbours and friends who have gathered for the occasion. Refreshments follow and the baby is given everyday foods to taste such as salt, pepper, palm oil and smoked fish.

In South Africa most birthdays include a feast of *Koeksisters* (see page 81), a special plaited cake dipped in a very sweet syrup; while in Switzerland a special birthday treat is a hot chocolate fondue (see page 82). In many countries the centre-piece to a birthday treat is a cake with candles on. The number of candles correspond with the age of the child and they have to be blown out in one blow!

Birthday books

The custom of keeping a book from birth through a child's early life, recording important events, such as the first step or the first word, is quite common. Many people carry this on only until all the baby things have been accomplished, but it could go on longer. One idea is to write a page at each birthday, sticking in an up-to-date photograph and listing the important events of that year. Maybe this could be done together with the child, as he or she may remember different occasions as being important. Another way to celebrate the year just past is to make a card with pictures and descriptions, and title it 'This is your year'.

SPECIAL BIRTHDAYS

Coming of age

Coming of age is usually celebrated with a big family party and this could be the appropriate time to hand over any childhood record or birthday book. If such a record has not been kept then maybe one could be compiled for this occasion, with relatives and friends contributing to it. This is an important milestone for parents and their children. Some recognition of it is important.

Growing up does not happen overnight, of course; it goes on through the

---

Chocolate Fondue
Switzerland

8 oz	225 g	8 squares	dark chocolate (semi-sweet baking chocolate)
¼ pint	150 ml	⅓ cup	cream
¼ tsp	¼ tsp	¼ tsp	ground cinnamon
¼ tsp	¼ tsp	¼ tsp	nutmeg
¼ tsp	¼ tsp	¼ tsp	ground cloves

Fresh fruit, cake and biscuits

METHOD

1 Grate the chocolate or break into small pieces.

2 Put the chocolate, cream and spices into a fondue pot.

3 Heat gently, stirring until smooth and well blended. Take care not to let the chocolate stick or burn.

4 Prepare a plate of fruit, cake or biscuits cut into bite-size pieces.

To serve each person you will need a long fork and a napkin. The idea is to stab a piece of fruit or cake on your fork and dip it into the hot chocolate fondue. Gorgeous! You do need napkins to catch the drips.

Monday's child
   is fair of face.
Tuesday's child
   is full of grace.
Wednesday's child
   is full of woe.
Thursday's child
   has far to go.
Friday's child
   is loving and giving.
Saturday's child
   works hard for a living.
But the child that is born
   on the Sabbath day
Is bonny and bright
   in every way.

Clock Cake

Prepare a cake following the recipe for the Maypole Cake and bake it in the same way. Decorate the top like the face of a clock. Cut out hands from coloured card and put them in place pointing to the number of the birthday being celebrated.

Marshmallow Float

For something quite different to drink at a party, try these.
This quantity is enough for 3 glasses

1 small carton strawberry yoghurt			
1 pint	*500 ml*	*2½ cups*	*cold milk*
2 marshmallows per glass			

METHOD

1 Whisk the yoghurt and the milk together.

2 Pour into glasses and float 2 marshmallows on top.

3 Chill before serving.

Name Cake

Prepare a cake following the recipe for the Maypole Cake (see page 60) but bake it in a tin about 8 × 8 in./ 20 × 20 cm. Cover with butter icing and decorate it with the names of those attending the party.

whole of life. But during the teenage years the process can be both painful and exciting, as a child matures into a young adult. In some cultures coming of age happens as young as thirteen; for example, Jewish boys when they become a *bar mitzvah*. But in many countries coming of age has become synonymous with the right to vote. The most common age for this in the Western world is eighteen. Austria and Sweden have a voting age of nineteen; in Switzerland, Norway and Denmark, it is twenty. In Scandinavia a civil ceremony is held for those reaching voting age. Town or city dignitaries preside at the Town Hall, a band plays and refreshments are served. The young people who have previously received instruction in civic responsibility are welcomed as adult voting members of the community.

Receiving the key of the door is one tradition associated with reaching adulthood. As many young people often have their own door key long before coming of age, this is usually done with key symbols on birthday cards or with cardboard replicas. I do remember, however, that my father had a key specially cut for my twenty-first birthday. In the United Kingdom the voting age was changed from twenty-one to eighteen only in 1969. This gives some young people a good excuse for two celebrations!

Here are some ideas for special birthday parties.

Tournament party

This party idea will keep boys of 9-10 years of age entertained. Ask your own children to get out all the games they enjoy playing. Only choose ones that can be completed in under 10 minutes — Monopoly is no good! Include simple board games, plenty of paper and pencils for noughts and crosses (tic tac toe), and packs of cards. If you have a computer then computer games will definitely prove popular. Some games — like darts or table tennis — will need adult supervision. Have all the games well distributed around the house (and garden if the weather is fine) and give each child a score card and an order of events. Get them to play in pairs or individually and move round the various games scoring as they go. The winner is the one with the most points at the end of the tournament. Maybe you could make gold, silver and bronze medals for the winners. You will have to work out a system for scoring that is easy and fair. Try to get games that are as varied as possible — some needing skill and some needing thought.

Hot potato party

This is an easy way of filling up hungry young people without involving you in too much work! Allow at least one potato per person. Cook the potatoes in good time in the oven Gas Mark 7/210°C/425°F for about an hour and a half or in small numbers in a microwave and keep them hot in the oven. Have plenty of fillings available for everyone to help themselves to. Here are a few suggestions:

CHICKEN AND SWEETCORN Mix some cooked chicken cut into small pieces with a tin of sweetcorn kernels.

TUNA IN MAYONNAISE Drain one or two tins of tuna and stir in enough mayonnaise to thoroughly coat the fish.

SAUSAGE AND BEANS Mix one or two cans of baked beans with a can of hot-dog sausages cut into small pieces.

BACON, ONION AND MUSHROOM Chop an onion into small pieces, slice some mushrooms and chop up several rashers of bacon, fry them all together until cooked. Drain on absorbent paper.

GRATED CHEESE This is best served on its own.

Have a bowl of green salad and a bowl of coleslaw available.

Follow with a simple fruit salad or prepare a selection of homemade sweets (candies) (see recipes for Gum Nut Chews, Peppermint Creams and Fruit and Nut Clusters on page 26/27).

WEDDINGS

For this reason a man will leave his father and mother and be united to his wife, and they will become one flesh.

GENESIS 2:24 New International Version

Marriage has its origins way back in the history of society. Traditions may vary in different cultures, and of course practices have changed over time, but the idea of leaving parents, being united with a new partner and setting up home are common to most traditions. Even if the home is set up with in-laws, the boundaries of responsibility and loyalty change from being directed towards parents to the new partner. There is a passage from an old state to a new one. There are many customs which symbolize this passage. Some form part of the marriage ceremony and some come in the festivities that follow the service.

A bride usually comes to the ceremony with her father who 'gives her away' to the bridegroom, who escorts her out. In church weddings the bride's guests often sit on one side of the church while the groom's guests sit on the other. As the wedding party leaves, the groom's father escorts the bride's mother and the bride's father the groom's mother, showing that now the families are united by marriage.

Rings are universally used as a sign of the never-ending quality of marriage. The exchange of rings (husband to wife, and wife to husband) is now more common than it once was. In an Orthodox church ceremony the couple wear crowns to symbolize that for that day they are king and queen — the occasion is a truly royal one.

Passing through a guard of honour forming an archway outside the church door is a symbol of going from the single state to the married one. A military guard of honour with drawn swords is common if either party is in the armed forces. Sometimes the guard represents an occupation or hobby — a gardener may be represented with hoes, a draughtsman with set-squares and so on.

There are other ways of symbolizing passing into a new state. On Holy Island in

Kourambiedhes Wedding Cakes

Greece

1 lb	450 g	4 cups	plain flour
4 oz	125 g	1/2 cup	sugar
8 oz	225 g	2 sticks	butter or margarine
2 tsp	2 tsp	2 tsp	vanilla essence (extract)
1/2	1/2	1/2	egg
2 tbsp	2 tbsp	2 tbsp	milk or brandy
4 oz	125 g	3/4 cup	roasted almonds, coarsely ground
			orange blossom water (if available)
			icing (confectioners) sugar

METHOD

1 Cream the butter and sugar together.

2 Add the vanilla, ground almonds, egg and milk and mix well.

3 Add the flour gradually and knead for a few minutes. Cover and let it stand for a while.

4 Put small mounds on a greased baking tray and bake in the oven at Gas Mark 6/200°C/400°F for about 15-20 minutes or until light brown.

5 Cool on a cooling tray.

6 When cool sprinkle with orange blossom water and dust with icing sugar.

Matrimony Cake

This recipe originates in the West Country of England but why it is called matrimony cake I do not know!

8 oz	225 g	1/2 lb	pastry
4 tbsp	4 tbsp	4 tbsp	brown breadcrumbs
4	4	4	large apples, peeled and cored
4 tbsp	4 tbsp	4 tbsp	mixed dried fruit
1/2 tsp	1/2 tsp	1/2 tsp	nutmeg
1/2 tsp	1/2 tsp	1/2 tsp	ginger
2 tbsp	2 tbsp	2 tbsp	sugar
2 tbsp	2 tbsp	2 tbsp	golden (corn) syrup
			juice of one lemon
			a slice of lemon

METHOD

1 Divide the pastry — two-thirds and one-third.

2 Roll out the two-thirds and line an 8 in./20 cm flan tin with the pastry.

3 Lay slices of apple in the pastry and put the other ingredients on top, finishing with the slice of lemon in the middle.

4 Top with the remaining pastry.

5 Bake in oven at Gas Mark 4/180°C/350°F for about 40 minutes or until the pastry is golden brown.

6 Serve hot with custard or cold with whipped cream.

Jesus the Lord of love and life,
draw near and bless this man and wife;
as they are now in love made one,
let your good will for them be done.

Give them each day your peace and joy,
let no dark clouds these gifts destroy;
in growing trust may love endure,
to keep their marriage-bond secure.

As they have vowed to have and hold,
each by the other be consoled;
in wealth or want, in health or pain,
till death shall part, let love remain.

Deepen, O Lord, their love for you,
and in that love, their own renew;
each in the other find delight,
as lives and interests now unite.

Be to them both a guide and friend,
through all the years their home defend;
Jesus the Lord of love and life,
stay near and bless this man and wife

JAMES E. SEDDON (1915-1983)
© Mavis Seddon/Jubilate Hymns

Wales the bride has to step over a 'petting stone' coming out of church. This shows she is leaving behind pet likes and tempers and stepping over into a new life. I'm not sure why the groom does not follow this custom too!

On the island of Karpathos in Greece the couple break a rod across the doorway, symbolizing going through and entering a new life. In Cleveland in the north of England the couple leap over a bench and in Somerset in England the church path is chained with a rope of flowers. In each case the picture is of going from one side to the other.

Noise is a traditional way of announcing the wedding to the world. Often church bells ring out and guns are fired if the couple are military or royalty. In America car horns are sounded, deafening all around. In country villages in England, in days past, the blacksmith would explode gunpowder on his anvil. In many countries fireworks provide the noise and excitement.

The first thing most couples do after the ceremony is to share a meal and have a wedding feast with their guests and friends. In America the couple feed each other with the first piece of wedding cake to express their oneness. In France the couple drink from a two-handled gold or silver *coupe de marriage*. This is often a gift engraved with their initials and the wedding date. In Orthodox church ceremonies the couple drink three times from a cup of wine, symbolizing their willingness to share the same experiences. The ancient Greeks shared a quince together to show that they were prepared to share all things both sweet and bitter. Greek brides sometimes carry a lump of sugar in their gloves to add sweetness to married life!

Wedding cakes, as we know them today, were introduced from France in the seventeenth century. Traditionally there were two cakes — the bride's cake, a light one decorated with spun sugar ornaments; and the groom's cake, which was a rich fruit one. Today there is usually just one cake, although this may consist of several tiers. In America, the bride's cake is favoured and is often a light lemon or chocolate-flavoured cake decorated with white icing. In England it is more common to have a rich fruit cake, decorated with white icing.

Until the nineteenth century special clothes were seldom bought and in many countries national costumes were worn. Before the days of the honeymoon holiday away from home, the couple went straight to their new home to begin married life and on the first Sunday following the wedding the couple would lead their family to church, dressed in their wedding clothes. This was known as 'coming-out bride' in America and 'showing-off Sunday' in England. They would arrive just as the service was about to begin, and take special seats very slowly so that everybody could admire their attire. In Ireland, Jersey and Guernsey there are similar customs. In some places the bride was allowed to choose the text for the sermon that day. In England the husband walked first into church to show who was master.

The most common custom showing the added responsibility which marriage brings is carrying the bride over the threshold. Another less kind tradition comes from Scotland and is called 'creeling'. The morning following the wedding, the husband is made to carry a 'creel' or basket full of stones. This represents the newly-assumed and weighty responsibilities acquired in marriage. He has to carry this burden around the town until released by a kiss from his bride. If she is shy or a bit of a tease her husband could have his burden for some time. The master of ceremonies at the 'creeling' is the last groom to have carried the burden so he is usually quite keen to see another suffer the same affliction.

One old custom that has now ceased is the giving of grave clothes at the time of marriage. This may seem a very strange item to include, but in days when death was never far away, it was not forgotten even at the time of marriage. In country areas of England in the last century it was

1st	Paper
2nd	Cotton
3rd	Leather
4th	Silk
5th	Wood
6th	Iron
7th	Wool
8th	Bronze
9th	Pottery
10th	Tin
15th	Crystal
20th	China
25th	Silver
30th	Pearl
35th	Coral
40th	Ruby
45th	Sapphire
50th	Gold
55th	Emerald
60th	Diamond

not uncommon for a bride to embroider a cross on her husband's wedding smock and put it away for him to be buried in. Sometimes a couple would give each other a set of grave clothes as wedding presents and these were put on show with all the other gifts. In Sweden a wedding shirt and in Spain a night shirt were common gifts to be put away for burial. Queen Victoria of England was buried with her face covered by her wedding veil.

In America and Canada bridal showers are very common. These will often take the form of a surprise party organized by friends of the bride. Everyone brings a gift for the new home. Often the young woman will have to do some sort of test to win each gift. This may be peeling an apple without breaking the skin or folding towels neatly in a given length of time. If the gifts have bows on them they are sometimes taken off and used to decorate a paper hat for the bride to wear, or attached to a paper plate which is used as the bouquet at the wedding rehearsal. Games may also be played such as seeing how many bridal words can be made out of the letters that make up the bride's name.

Sometimes young men getting married are given a 'honey-do' shower by their friends. They receive gifts of dusters, brushes, aprons, and so on, with the command 'honey-do this' and 'honey do that'.

So far we have only looked at the wedding day itself, but of course marriage is for life.

I, N, take you, N,
to my wife/husband,
to have and to hold
from this day forward,
for better, for worse,
for richer, for poorer,
in sickness and in health,
to love and to cherish,
till death us do part,
according to God's holy law;
and this is my solemn vow.
from the marriage service
in *The Alternative Service Book* 1980

A young man looking through these words at a marriage preparation session said, 'These should be printed and put up somewhere in every home as a daily reminder of the promises we make.' What a good idea! Several passages in the Bible compare Christ's self-giving love for the church to the love two people share within marriage. So we should celebrate marriage. Of course, we do on the wedding day, but then what? We all know old jokes about husbands forgetting their wedding anniversary. We laugh as if it doesn't matter. If the love of a husband and wife is a picture of Christ's love for the church, then it does matter and we should want to remember.

A lovely custom for remembering comes from America. At their wedding some couples are given a tall white memory candle. It is scented with lily-of-the-valley, which is often used as a wedding flower, and lit first at the wedding reception. Thereafter it is lit every wedding anniversary and is intended to last through to the Golden Wedding.

The German custom of celebrating anniversaries with various commodities is now practised worldwide.

The items get more precious as the years go by, not in a way of a prize for endurance but to recognize the growing richness of marriage as it deepens with the years.

There are many ancient — and rather eccentric — English customs relating to marriage. For example, records dating back to 1445 tell of this old custom still practised in the town of Dunmow in Essex. A 'flitch' or side of bacon is given to any couple who can swear that they have not 'repented' their marriage for a year and a day. The oath has to be sworn in traditional words before 'a jury of maidens and bachelors'. Records also tell of one man who definitely repented of his marriage. In 1832 in Carlisle Market a farmer sold his wife who was described as 'a born serpent' and a 'domestic curse'. He did acknowledge, however, that she could milk cows, read novels, make butter, scold maids and sing. He got twenty shillings and a Newfoundland dog for her! Fortunately the custom of wife-selling went out of fashion in Britain during the nineteenth century.

Looking at the vows made to each other on your wedding day is a very good way of checking your progress as a couple. How about writing a letter to each other on an anniversary, looking back over the last year? You could list important events, say thank you for the good things and sorry for the things you regret. Having read the letters, acknowledge to each other what you have said by receiving the thanks and accepting the apologies. It may be right to set some targets for the coming year. This could be shared over a special meal together either at home or at a restaurant.

Almighty God, our heavenly Father, who gave marriage to be a source of blessing to mankind, we thank you for the joys of family life. Pour out upon us your Holy Spirit, that we may truly love and serve you. Bless all who are married and every parent and child. May we know your presence and peace in our homes; fill them with your love and use them for your glory; through Jesus Christ, our Lord. Amen.

Part of the Mothers' Union Prayer

Although a couple celebrating a wedding anniversary need time on their own, the children should be drawn in somewhere. After all, they are the product of love and marriage. Looking through the wedding photographs with the family can be fun. Children do need to realize that there was a time before they existed, when parents were young and didn't have grey hair. Young children find this hard to understand so it has to be done gently. They probably will not like to be laughed at if they ask where they were when the wedding photographs were taken. Talking through the event can help them to understand and to share in the joy we feel about that very special occasion.

BABY'S BIG DAY

Along with all the family celebrations to welcome a new baby, many parents want to express their faith in God at this special time. They want to declare their intention to bring the child up as a Christian within the family of the church and they do this in a service of Infant Baptism (Christening) or Dedication.

Baptism has been practised since the beginning of the Christian church and goes back to Peter's words in his first sermon on the day of Pentecost, recorded in the Acts of the Apostles: 'Repent and be baptized every one of you in the name of Jesus Christ for the forgiveness of sins; and you shall receive the gift of the Holy Spirit. For the promise is to you and your children and to all that are far off, every one whom the Lord our God calls to him.'

The parents choose three Godparents or sponsors and together, after declaring their own faith in Christ and rejection of evil, they promise to bring the child up as a Christian within the family of the church. The baby is signed with the sign of the cross on his or her forehead and then baptized with water in the name of the Father, the Son and the Holy Spirit. In some churches the parents are given a lighted candle for the baby, to show that the child has passed from darkness to light and is then welcomed into the Christian family of the church. The candle is taken home and lit on each anniversary of the baptism and sometimes a prayer for the growing Christian life of the child will be said.

In the service of Dedication parents thank God for the safe arrival of the baby and the safe delivery for the mother, and also for the joy and privilege of joining with God in the act of creation. They will dedicate the child to God as Hannah, childless for many years, dedicated Samuel to the Lord in the Old Testament. 'I asked God for this child and he gave me what I asked for. So I am dedicating him to the Lord. As long as he lives, he will belong to

Croquembouche
France

PASTRY BASE:

2 oz	50 g	½ cup	flour
1 oz	25 g	1 tbsp	butter or margarine
1 oz	25 g	⅛ cup	sugar
1	1	1	egg yolk

CHOUX PASTRY:

½ pint	250 ml	1 cup	water
4 oz	100 g	½ cup	butter or margarine
5 oz	150 g	1¼ cups	flour
4	4	4	eggs
3-4 tbsp	3-4 tbsp	3-4 tbsp	finely chopped almonds
2-3 tbsp	2-3 tbsp	2-3 tbsp	icing (or confectioners) sugar
			egg wash — a little beaten egg in 2 tbsp milk

SYRUP:

6 oz	175 g	¾ cup	sugar
5 tbsp	5 tbsp	5 tbsp	water
			pinch of cream of tartar

DECORATION:

Halved glacé cherries and pieces of angelica or hard-sugar cake decorations

This dessert can either be filled with or served with cream and fruit, or eaten as it is.

METHOD: Pastry Base

1 Rub the butter into the flour and add the sugar.

2 Mix to a soft dough with the egg yolk and roll into a circle about 8 in./20 cm across.

3 Bake in oven Gas Mark 5/190°C/375°F for 15-20 minutes or until golden brown.

4 Allow to cool.

METHOD: Choux Buns

1 Sift the flour on to a piece of paper.

2 Put water and butter into pan over heat, and bring slowly to the boil.

3 Take pan from heat and pour all the flour in once, stirring vigorously until the mixture is smooth.

4 Cool mixture for 5 minutes, then beat in the eggs one at a time. Beat mixture for about 3 minutes until it looks glossy.

5 Put mixture into a piping bag with a plain ½ in./1½ cm nozzle.

6 Pipe small even-sized balls on to a damped baking tray. Brush lightly with egg-wash; sprinkle with chopped nuts and dust with icing sugar.

7 Bake in a hot oven Gas Mark 7/220°C/425°F for about 20 minutes until firm and crisp.

8 Remove and put on to a cooling tray.

FOR SYRUP, AND TO ASSEMBLE THE CROQUEMBOUCHE:

1 Dissolve half the sugar in half the water over a low heat.

2 Add a pinch of cream of tartar and boil rapidly until it is a golden colour. Stop the boiling by placing the bottom of the pan in cold water.

3 Take a ball of choux and dip one side into the syrup and stick it onto the pastry base about ½ in./1½ cm from the edge. Stick all the balls together in a circle. Then put another row of balls on top of the first row and so on. When the syrup is used up, make up the second batch with the remaining ingredients.

4 If you are filling the centre of the tower with cream and fruit, remember to do this before the opening gets too narrow. Any left over syrup can be carefully dripped on to the finished tower.

5 Decorate with cherries and angelica. You can also pipe cream stars on to the croquembouche.

the Lord.' In the service of dedication parents also dedicate themselves to the child and make a vow to bring up the child and to teach him or her about the things of God. All the church members join in by promising their support by prayer, practical help and encouragement.

The Infant Baptism or Dedication service will usually be followed by a party for family and friends to rejoice together. In France sugared almonds are given to all the guests. It is a tradition in Britain that the top tier of a wedding cake is carefully kept for this occasion. The rich fruit cake matures with keeping, but the icing does not and so the cake does have to be re-iced. If you haven't got any left-over wedding cake how about trying this *Croquembouche* for an unusual centre piece for your Christening buffet? This attractive tower of tiny choux buns comes from France and is a traditional centre piece for a special party.

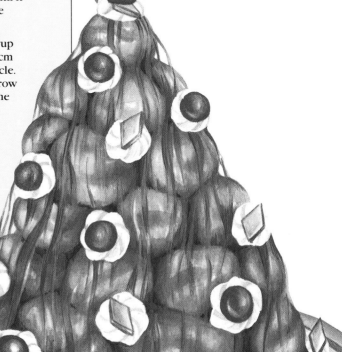

Confirmation and Adult Baptism

We should not forget Confirmation and Adult Baptism in this section. Both of these are special services for adults to confirm their faith and publicly declare their commitment to God and the church. In churches where Infant Baptism is the practice then Confirmation follows. Having been brought up in the family of the church, and coming to know Jesus Christ, his forgiveness and his love, a young person acknowledges publicly that he or she wants to go on in the Christian life. They 'confirm' the promises made on their behalf at baptism. In churches where Dedication is the pattern, Adult Baptism (or Believer's Baptism) is an opportunity for an individual to make a public declaration of faith in Jesus Christ. They are completely immersed in water (the church will have a baptistry — a large water tank, like a small swimming pool), and come out at the other side where they are greeted by representatives of the church. Being immersed in water and rising up from it symbolizes being 'buried' with Christ, and rising up to a new life in Christ, turning from an old way of life to start a new way and being 'cleansed' by the water.

Often the young adults are given gifts to commemorate this special occasion. A Bible, a cross and chain or a prayer book are the most popular gifts. But perhaps the best gift of all is your company at church services and your continued interest and prayers. Here's a prayer you can use.

Defend, O Lord, your servant with your heavenly grace,
that he/she may continue yours for ever,
and daily increase in your Holy Spirit more and more,
until he/she comes to your everlasting kingdom.
Amen

from the Confirmation Service in The *Alternative Service Book* 1980

Answers

1 : 42 **2** : 3 **3** : 6 **4** : 3 **5** : 84 **6** : 6 **7** : 12 (Immanuel, Jesus, Messiah, King of the Jews, Christ, Son of David, Son of Abraham, Son of the Most High, Son of God, Lord, Saviour, Nazarene). **8** : 4 **9** : 5 **10** : 8

INDEX

93